CW01333574

Hey Teacher, You're 'aving a Larf

Lawrence Gordon

authorHOUSE®

AuthorHouse™ UK Ltd.
500 Avebury Boulevard
Central Milton Keynes, MK9 2BE
www.authorhouse.co.uk
Phone: 08001974150

© *2008 Lawrence Gordon. All rights reserved.*

No part of this book may be reproduced, stored in a retrieval system, or transmitted by any means without the written permission of the author.

First published by AuthorHouse 3/25/2008

ISBN: 978-1-4343-6056-4 (sc)

Printed in the United States of America
Bloomington, Indiana

This book is printed on acid-free paper.

Thanks

Many thanks to the following who have supported me for most of my life and made contributions to my work, in particular whilst writing this book: Stewart Cooper, John and Helen Mitchell, Pam Bevan and my wife, Avril. The following school-friends also helped me, and my thanks go to Gill Griffiths, Malcolm Jacobs and Allan Bradshaw.

To my family, who have stood by me through thick and thin, I can only say thanks for being patient. Thanks to Merrie, my cocker spaniel, who helped walk me back to better health and has been, without doubt, one of my best friends.

Thanks to Helen Foster for her help, skill and contribution in writing this book.

Finally, thanks to Mindy Gibbins-Klein who motivated me to write my first book, 'Andrew, give us a Kiss', and to carry on and continue writing.

Table of Contents

Foreword	ix
The Early Days	1
Wilson Close	6
The Hospital	24
Primary School and the Start of Formal Education	35
Secondary Education	47
College and a Taste of Independence	61
Learning to Teach: Part One	90
Learning to Teach: Part Two	113
After School Activities	160

Foreword

The book chronicles a mere fraction of the fun experienced by myself, a retired schoolteacher, who was lucky enough to teach in the Sixties, Seventies, Eighties and Nineties. It includes tales about my own education, in school and college, and a snapshot of my life, as a schoolteacher, on the north-east side of Birmingham. It is not the type of book that is suitable for a PGCE course!

My parents, both now dead, were George Harry Gordon and Doris Eileen Gordon, who both came from the same small coal-mining town of Goldthorpe, between Barnsley and Doncaster in South Yorkshire. I have two sisters: Helen, born 1st October 1948 and Pamela, born May 29th 1950.

My own upbringing taught me many things and, in particular, one very hard fact of life which I feel is still relevant to this day. It is this: no-one knows what transpires behind closed doors. For me and my two sisters, many were the times we wished someone else DID know. Our family life was not always as it could have been, or should have been, in developing young adults. Tensions in the home were common place, as the most influential people in our lives, our parents, were constantly at each others throats, arguing. Despite all that, and because of it, we three children found an escape route in each others' company, outside of the house, to relieve the bitterness and fear we experienced in it. We never knew what type of confrontation would develop once our parents encountered each other again, after they each returned from their shift-work at the local hospital. It seemed only pot luck decided whether or not further arguments would take place over the most trivial issues.

Fortunately, we were able to find enjoyment and distractions elsewhere. We enjoyed our time together as brother and sisters. We immersed ourselves in our schooling and in sport and that is, I hope, reflected in the lives we have lead since those days. We were always able to laugh and joke, have fun together and find something to amuse us, even in the tensions we encountered at home. Our parents were far from being bad people, they just did not get on together, and that frightened us as young children. The War had impacted directly and personally on their lives through several family bereavements, and so our parents, like many others after the War, made sure that our generation had more of everything, consumer-wise, than any other preceding generation. To achieve this they worked long, hard hours towards that aim, or like our mum, simply went without the basic essentials of food or clothing and gave everything to her children. Consequently, there were tensions in the home.

The book shares with the reader events and incidents in my life that have created fun and laughter along the way.

The Early Days

Being born at the end of one of the most violent and destructive wars in history enabled my generation to have unparalleled comforts and a life so very unlike that experienced by our parents. We could almost have been from a different planet. In the Sixties, many of my contemporaries appeared to have done just that, because the way they acted and behaved seemed alien to any previous generation.

I suppose that when I was born and World War Two had finished in Europe, my parents, along with many other new parents, were optimistic and expectant for the future. We "Baby Boomers" had more money lavished on us than any other generation, not only by our families, but also by the Attlee Government elected after the Second World War. Council houses, hospitals, schools and travel infrastructure were all to be modernised, particularly in the cities that had suffered from aerial bombing. Virtually every adult seemed to have a job in those days. Rationing of all types continued well into the Fifties before it disappeared, as did what was known as Austerity Britain. Goods became less scarce as affluence among people increased.

I began life in Jessop's Hospital, Sheffield, in South Yorkshire at 04.30am on 20th October 1945. Many years later, on the other side of the world, I met an elderly lady doctor who claimed she may well have been at my birth. I shall return to that lady in another chapter. After two days in Jessop's Hospital I went with my mother, Doris, to live with Nana Swindells at Windermere Avenue, Goldthorpe, a small mining town between Doncaster and Rotherham. I have little recollection of those early years, except that photographs from that time show me well wrapped up against the harsh winter of 1947 often standing by the garden gate studying heaps of coal put there by the Coal Board. That was a tradition 'up north' for recently widowed ladies whose husbands had worked "Down t'pit" and sadly my Grandad had died two months before I was born.

As Britain recovered after the war, my father George, having been de-mobbed from the army, returned to civilian life, and to the job he had just begun before he volunteered to join up as war broke out. That job he had at the Pastures Hospital, near Derby, where he was a male nurse in a very large psychiatric hospital. He resided in living quarters at the Nurses' home in the hospital, but regularly travelled back to Yorkshire on his days off, not only to see his wife and son, but also his parents, who lived in the same town.

I was to learn much later from my dad that, around this time in 1946, something was not quite as it should have been at Windermere Avenue - that there was an 'atmosphere' in the house and it was not beneficial to my mum having just given birth to me. This resulted in my parents whisking me off to a set of two rooms in Abbey Street, Derby. My bed was a drawer in a chest of drawers! How high up I was in that chest of drawers I have no idea, but what I do know was that the attempt by my parents to start off on their own and find a home independent of their parents was soon doomed. Many years later, and after my mother had died, dad told me that mum suffered from what is now called post-natal depression. During that time mum was very ill. She was unable to cope with a new baby in a small bed-sit all day and really needed medical support, other than from my dad, which, of course, was not forthcoming. As her depression worsened mum threatened suicide and was going to kill me too, so my dad quickly upped sticks and took us back to Windermere Avenue and the hoped for 'comfort' in South Yorkshire. Dad returned to the Nurses' home at the hospital to keep the family finances ticking over.

In 1947-8 my parents were offered a house in Egginton, near Burton-on-Trent, on a disused airfield. For house, substitute Nissen hut. When mum and dad moved all their worldly goods, by open lorry, from Yorkshire to the Nissen hut in Egginton, mum and I travelled in the cab with the driver and dad on the back of the open lorry. If that wasn't bad enough for him, he sat amongst a ton and a half of coal that his father, Grandad Gordon, had given us to keep us warm through the coming winter. My dad travelled the whole distance, on top of the coal, with his legs dangling over the back of the lorry! What would "elf and safety" say today?

Listening to my parents talk of life in Egginton you'd have thought they had won the Pools, as they now relaxed in the comfort of their own home. Cold, drab and austere are words that spring to my mind when I think of those times in that hut. The fact that over the next 20 years or so Egginton virtually disappeared from family conversations as we had moved house again, suited me fine. Other families rented the vacated ex-air force Nissen huts if the father worked at the Pastures Hospital. Male nurses, returning from their shift-work at the hospital, often raced home on their bicycles, a distance of five miles. No wonder obesity was unheard of in those days. Only the occasional bus or doctor's car would slow them down in the pursuance of their 'yellow jersey'. We children would often wander off to play in the vast expanse that became our playground: the old runways and tarmac of the aerodrome. Moving outside the perimeter of the estate, we regularly wandered off, safely, into the surrounding countryside ... and we were still under five years of age! Surprised to find a Billy goat in an adjacent field all by himself one afternoon, yours truly went to stroke him on his head that had large horns. The story goes that the goat immediately charged at me, with his head down, butted me over a low hedge nearby, and dumped me heavily on my bum. Where were my mates at that moment? Good question.

In the summer of that same year, several of us little explorers, wandering by a canal with some older children, came across some swans. You've got it. Again, yours truly went to pat a nice swan on his head. Wham! An early bath in the canal and a battering by the swans resulted in me being badly bruised, but I was rescued this time, by my friends. Naturally, rollickings were in order from parents and we never went near the canal again till years later.

A good start to life then: sleeping in a drawer, almost a victim of infanticide, making friends with a goat and practising Swan Lake with real swans! All before I was four years old too! Looking back to those times, and listening to the recollections of friends who were with me at the time, it seems obvious that my life was never going to be dull. How right that is: my life has been packed with fun and laughter, whether at school, college, teaching, university, in sport, with my family or with friends and acquaintances. There has rarely been a dull moment. There has, of course, been the occasional heartache too, let me kid you not. But life has been good, richly rewarding and fun.

Wilson Close

In 1948 a new housing estate was built near the hospital where dad worked and was named Wilson Close. Jumping at the offer of a brand new house, they, we, moved in and mum and dad were to celebrate again nine months later in the October of 1948 when my sister, Cynthia Helen was born – with five fingers AND a thumb on each hand! Pianist she isn't, but having had the fifth fingers removed, she became a brilliant performer on the recorder. I was often to wonder later if she would have been even better on the recorder with the extra fingers.

Wilson Close. Those were the days, so they say, and that was the start of how we came to live in a community within a community. Kids of all ages were everywhere, playing on the vast, grassy oval and safe perimeter road in Wilson Close. Young dads, back from the war, worked off any extra energy with skill in the nearby allotments,

Hey Teacher, You're 'aving a Larf

after shift work at the hospital. Mums took advantage of new and large gardens to fill their washing lines every Monday, the sacrosanct washing day. Children went to school, came home and played, often in the dark, in the safety of this environment. Heaven? Well it was to me.

14 Wilson Close was now to be my home until I went to college in Birmingham in 1964. The house that was three bed-roomed and semi-detached consisted of a separate lounge and dining room, a large kitchen, bathroom and separate toilet upstairs. Oh, and an airing cupboard. My parents really must have thought they had won the pools. (Years later my father did win the pools, £750.00p to be precise, and bought a television with some of the money. At the Queen's Coronation in 1953, there were thirty five adults and children in our house - me thinks shades of India!) Outside was the coalhouse, outside loo with the customary newspaper toiletry - very much needed - and gardens back and front. The front flower garden saw more cricket balls, tennis balls and footballs in it over the years than most sports stadiums. The back garden had a lawn (for practising ball games, naturally) and a vegetable patch that, along with the allotment, provided the whole family with fresh produce throughout the year, and plenty of good hidings for me when I chose to sample the fruit!

My own bedroom would have been easily recognisable from the outside until I was about 8 years old, because the curtains were made of blackout material from the recent War. What my parents were trying to prove I have no idea since I never did see any German aeroplanes as I peeked out of them. I did think I heard the Germans somewhere around when I couldn't get to sleep at night, but I think they worked at the hospital. The blackouts worked though, because it was often before 7 o'clock when my sisters and I went to bed, even on a summer evening, when all the other kids in the Close were still out playing. Some years later, when I was 12, and in grammar school, my parents completely refurbished my bedroom and took away the World War Two blackout curtains. No more Germans then, just a new bed, new linen, new carpet, new flowery-patterned curtains for a boy, oh, and of course new wallpaper to transform that former bunker of mine. Those curtains played havoc with my imagination over next few years, as their patterns reflected various faces, bodies or vehicles that put my youthful imagination into overdrive as I lay there awake. The battles I fought, and won, against the imaginary enemies and midnight attackers I saw in those shapes in the curtains, saved my family from mortal danger as I was growing older, or more stupid.

In the right hand corner of the bedroom was a built-in wardrobe that housed my beloved, electric Hornby Doublo train-set, the pride of all my toys. Many times I took a piece of that train-set to bed with me and chuff-chuffed myself to sleep, before I was wakened in darkness with a coupling or guard's wagon sticking somewhere in my body! I remember the year I had that train-set was 1950. I couldn't get near it for my dad. If I did, I had to let go of the transformer if my dad thought I'd had a long enough go, stopping and starting Sir Nigel Gresley as it sped round the track!

Then he'd be back for another go himself. The train-set gave me endless hours of fun, particularly on a wet day, and kept me out of trouble for years, until I started train-spotting. I was really surprised years later, when I found out my Nana Swindells had bought the set for me, because my male cousins already had a set and my parents couldn't afford one at that time.

Life had settled into that cosy rhythm of going to school, coming home and playing outside. In the summer we always played outside before, and after, teatime. In winter, we played outside if the light allowed, or under a lamp-post until teatime, then we might stay in and listen to the radio or read a book. What 'radio times' we had in those days. 'Dick Barton, Special Agent' with Jock Anderson and Snowy White I can just about remember, with its audience of about 15 million listeners at the time. My favourite, without doubt though, was 'Journey into Space' with Jet Morgan, Doc Matthews, Mitch and Lemmy my favourites. Years later I found that the actors playing those parts were to become household names on TV: David Kossoff, Alfie Bass, Andrew Faulds, Derek Guyler and even David Jacobs. My favourite books in those days included 'Biggles', 'Famous Five', 'Secret Seven' and an American intruder, 'The Bobsey Twins'. All these, whether book or radio, stimulated the imaginations in many kids. I sometimes wonder if today's kids are missing out on developing their imaginations as so many seem to skip childhood, going from breast or bottle feeding straight into long trousers!!

In the 'Close' the interaction between the children, and the adults who lived and worked at the hospital, was more like a large family than neighbours. Sure, some were not so good with their inter-personal skills and kept to themselves, but they would all gather together at certain times of the year. For the children, friendships were formed and broken through play and games. In summer and winter we played games outside someone's house, in a house, at a house's gate, on the road, on the field, and even by the sand-pit which was situated in the middle of the Close and was the venue for the annual bonfire night

Some of the games we played included hopscotch; 'Queenie-Queenie who's got the ball?'; skipping, with short and long ropes; hide- and- seek; cricket at the gate; football; tennis 'over' the gate 'net'; six bricks and, of course, when the grass was long, Lions and Tigers. Inside the house, my sisters and friends played 'mummies and daddies'; 'doctors and nurses'(and when they were much older too!); 'shops', which was where Helen, the elder sister, was always the shop-keeper taking the money (nothing changes); hide and seek; hide the thimble and hide Pam's doll, Diana. 'Bus Conductors' was a game played on our stairs and was to introduce Helen to the entrepreneurial skills she has improved yearly. Complete with ticket machine, Helen actually charged, and relieved Pam of her pocket money, to travel on her bus! All games we played until we were too tired or someone felt cheated in the game and arguments started. Worse still, until someone's parent called their child home for dinner or tea. In those days it was always dinner and tea in that order, never lunch and dinner as it is today. How times move on. In those days, too, we always sat down together as a family to eat our meals, which is very different from many homes today.

More play developed on the circular road that went all the way round the Close like a natural race track, which, of course, it became. This racing began firstly with three-wheeler bikes, then two-wheeler bikes and eventually, when we were young men, motor bikes and scooters. Did I mention that this race track was not the sole prerogative of children? Indeed, parents regularly raced their sons and daughters or other parents around the track! That was the type of friendship I referred to when I said that a family atmosphere permeated the whole ethos of Wilson Close. My own three-wheeler bike though, for what it is worth was a Four Aces bike. A Four Aces bike I hear you say, and what was special about that? Well, it had pneumatic tyres for a start, which were not always on other kid's three-wheelers, and it came complete with a pair of legs that were like whirlwinds and only ever, ever lost races round that track to two-wheeler bikes! Yep, my legs pumped like dynamos as the tyres whirred round, my sisters cheering me onwards, upwards ……….

I lived in a completely different world as a child, and only now realise how lucky those of us were that lived in the Close. This involved playing lots of football, cricket and tennis all of which became my passion. Cricket played against any gate or wall in the Close, or at school, I played from morn until dusk, and even then by the light of a lamp post, from the age of four till I was eighteen. The 'centre' of the Close to the right of the sand-pit had a large expanse of grass that was divided in two by the road and appeared again onto the 'curved' football pitch on the other side. We created a cricket pitch, cut and rolled just it like Trent Bridge, and used it every night in summer. The younger children played first because they were home from school early and then the older secondary school age children also joined in to bat and bowl. Fifteen or twenty aside on the pitch at the same time was not uncommon and included parents too. We could never understand how the England Test teams were losing matches in those days, not when our 'England' never lost a game in Wilson Close. We only ever came off and finished the game when the night was pitch-black and the already darkened ball had become invisible. I remember well one night, after tea, I was left standing holding my bat all alone, the hard, wizened cricket ball at my feet as everyone else had gone home early. Just because I was 207 not out and I was only eleven years of age. Later that night, at the dining room table, I completed my quintuple century, long before Brian Lara scored his, using my metal "Owzat" cricket game, and eventually fell asleep happy and content.

On another occasion, playing cricket with my mate Rod on our pitch, I created mayhem with the cricket ball but never saw the result of my efforts at that precise moment. Rod would keep bowling on my leg-side which as any fellow left-hander will tell you is, well, meat and drink. As one ball too many ventured on the leg side, I thought I'd finally show him how far I could really hit the ball. Lifting my "sawn-off" Jack Robertson bat and striking the ball, I crashed it to the leg-side high in the air, over the road, over a garden and into ....there, watching TV peacefully in his lounge (front room) before he went to work, was my dad's mate from Blackburn, Bob Smith. However, seeing the flight of the ball through the air, and where it looked like landing, Rod and I took off at full speed. Rod happened to live next door to the Smiths and so soon arrived at his gate and sanctuary, whereas I lived further up the Close, had further to run, and just managed to pass our gate when the ball went through the window and smashed Bob Smith's telly! Bob Smith must have dashed out from his house, looked out over his gate only to see an empty field that had in the middle of it four wickets, a bat and not a cricketer in sight. It was a breathless young man who had to explain to his father why he was so out of breath at that second, and why he'd run home so quickly. It was the same ever so apologetic young man, watched by his father, who went to the Smiths to say "Sorry for the broken telly Mr Smith, but can I have my ball back please, because it was me that broke your window?"

Oh the trials of life. Bob Smith must have felt sorry for me because some weeks later, against his gate and over two nights, I scored my absolutely most massive and highest ever innings of 339 not out and was forced to retire! My own sporting heroes at that time, as an eleven year old, were not only the England players, but two local lads who lived in the Close, Malcolm Heaver and Peter Anstey. Both were at least five years older than me and gifted at most sports, but mainly cricket and football. Malcolm was exceptionally good at cricket and kept wicket for Derbyshire Under-15's, and had a real cricket-bag at the time too, and his own bat. Was I jealous?

Malcolm and Peter both had fathers who were male nurses at the same hospital as my own father. Many other families that were influential in and around the Close included: the Bucks, Wybers, Divers, 2 sets of Smiths, Severns, Lilley, Slaney, Thompson, Tomlinson, Trumper and Longden, male nurses, engineers or upholsterers all of them. This group of families was my life-blood, or rather their sons and daughters were. In this same Close, houses were available for doctors and, at various times, included Drs Tyner, Taylor, Gunn and Dunne. The Matron of the hospital lived in the Close too, and if you hit or kicked a ball into her garden you had to wait until dark to retrieve it, carefully.

My immediate and close buddies included names like some American film: Rod, "Fats", "Gongy", Denny, "Keggy", "Mingus", Martin, Colin, Charlie and Kev to name most of them. There were others whose names escape me, and I must apologise if I have forgotten to mention someone. With some pals it was sport; with others the more devious pursuits of scrumping, air-rifle shooting, trespassing across farms or playing with trains. Later, as we all grew older, the friends were to include "outsiders" that lived away from the Close: Chris, Mickey, James and Jimmy. Similarly, as I grew older, I started to move to pastures new for sport, or the girls, as we all did. New territory was to bring with it new challenges.

From being five to twelve years old the majority of my time, as I've said, was spent playing football and cricket with the occasional lapse in June when almost everyone was playing tennis, copying their Wimbledon heroes of course! Football boots became important even for a seven year-old. A soft toe-cap on the boot was a must, as were brilliantly white laces washed so many times they went mouldy or brown. The dubbing was important too, especially if you wanted to impress mates and of course a full set of leather studs were paramount. My football shorts were perched high on my thorax the elastic cutting into my ribs and they hung down so low past my knees that it appeared I played without socks! Mother's sartorial appreciation of all things football never ever got off the ground. If that wasn't enough because having been 'dressed' so to speak, one had to 'walk the walk' in those confounded boots with those studs. My little legs would go in all directions like Bambi on ice whilst the young footballer had to negotiate concrete or tarmac on the way to the pitch. But once there .... oh heck! Nana and mum on the touchline telling me to avoid the puddles in the pitch as I'd catch a cold if I fell over into one. And this was only my first game for the senior school side aged seven! What on earth would I contract if I played till I was twelve, or even longer? Nothing as it turned out, but they did watch me play most games till I went to grammar school.

Returning home from school did not always involve sport, but playing outside always did when possible and the weather allowed. Sitting on a cold brick-based lamp-post, (I'd catch worms through my trousers if I sat on cold bricks my Nan said), and chatting to my friends, walking across open fields, organising a picnic down the "Wall Side", pitching a tent and smuggling sweets in to eat and share with friends, going scrumping or shooting air rifles were all part of our fun, not all with parental knowledge I can assure you. Even in those days farmers were not keen on you crossing their land to get to a barn in which you would play Cowboys and Indians. The thrill, however, of thinking you were being spied on by the farmer just heightened the excitement and adventure, sending your heart racing as you scurried across his land. If he saw you and let off a stream of expletives in your direction, or the occasional shot gun, reversing your run across his land in one movement, it seemed you were able to run away from him twice as fast. Well that is how it seemed at the time. Perhaps it was just that the heart beat faster or that one's bowels were ready to explode.

Picnics were even more fun when my mother thought I was old enough to venture more than a mile away from the house! I feel that if I hadn't persisted when I did, she would have prevented me from picnicking with mates even now. The fun of eating a squashed and slightly warm egg sandwich, and later, the new trendy sandwich spread, all washed down with NHS orange juice – barely discoloured water I seem to remember – with a cork sticking out of the bottle, finished off with a melted bar of chocolate that had been stuck in your back pocket, transported us kids into 'Never-Never Land'. Until that was, the hospital farm bailiff appeared from nowhere, asked us for our names and addresses and then told us in no uncertain manner to 'Bugger off, you cheeky beggars.' No sense of humour that bailiff, especially when he would not accept that Mickey Mouse and Donald Duck lived just down the road from him! It could have been worse for the bailiff. After the harvest, the baler left the bales all round the fields and we kids would seldom miss the opportunity to corral them into a defensive fort. So he was lucky we kept the 'invaders' off his land.

Then there were the army tents, surplus to requirements, purloined no doubt by some returning soldier to the hospital ranks, subsequently acquired by a son or daughter and pitched on the grass on the Close field. On a hot summer's day the tents were insufferable. The heat that was generated in them was difficult to describe in words when they were empty, but with 10-12 children in them, telling jokes, learning to swear and showing each other body parts, they could have been major health hazards! Sleeping overnight in one of those tents meant that the following morning, when parents were aware of the return of their prodigal, the said child had to undergo the human equivalent of the sheep-dip. Translating, a good soaking in the bath followed by a scrubbing with green or red carbolic soap would definitely discourage the child from entering into the tent's void overnight ever again.

One of the doctor's sons was, until I went to grammar school, my best mate. Sadly for me he was to leave the Close and go to live up north in Lancashire, but we had shed loads of fun before he left. A talented sportsman, he always challenged my abilities, often getting the better of me. One Xmas he had a pellet gun as a present, something that I would never be able to have, but was always envious of. What he could do to tin cans with that rifle facing forwards, backwards or with it stuck between his legs using a mirror, would certainly have rivalled Kit Carson at that time. Those tricks with a rifle he taught me too, and, of course, I would go home and brag to my sisters about my experiences with the gun, they called me Hopalong Cassidy because I had been out shooting. And, as sure as eggs are eggs, my parents would pounce on me wanting to know "Where, why, when, how?" was I involved with a rifle, as parents did, and still do. Is nothing secret?

One of the highlights of the year where I lived was the November 5th Bonfire Night. Weeks before the big day every scrap of wood, branch, tree trunk or tree was lifted towards the sand-pit in the middle of the Close's field by all those who could carry them. That was one other reason why we were often shouted at by farmers, for lugging wood across their fields. This major operation was helped by the October school's half-term just prior to the bonfire night. Most of the children helped fetch wood as the elder ones built and stacked the bonfire professionally, they insisted, to give the fire a good burn. On the night before Bonfire Night, euphemistically called Mischief Night, anything could and did happen around the houses in our Close. I lost count of the number of times the treacle went missing from our kitchen pantry but mysteriously finished up smeared on the toilet seats of most of the outside loos of people in the Close who had forgotten to lock them! Then there were broken jam jars smashed outside a house, whilst a cotton-bobbin was scraped up and down the nearest window to simulate a broken pane of glass. Or my favourite, the rat up a drainpipe which was the burning rubbish and paper howling through the metal drain pipe sounding like a steam train. Back in those days we seemed to have more frosts than we have today and therefore, to stay warm, we would nick any large tin can found lying around, bore holes in it and then go round with a small fire in it, twigs alight and swinging it round on thick string like a lantern. On a cold night they were very useful, and a welcome accompaniment, as we went about our mischief. Most of us attended the large bonfire after small firework displays in our own gardens. Parents came along too and we all congregated near the bonfire, normally lit at about seven o'clock on the night by some older urchin or parent. Fireworks would go off all over the place, no cohesion, just light them there and then, and retire. Treacle toffee, if any treacle escaped Mischief Night, was handed round by philanthropic mothers. So too, as we grew older, were toffee apples and drinks for the adults and parents! In all honesty, of all the Bonfire Nights I attended in the Close not one 'single-pingle' event resulted in an accident of any kind that I remember.

Another experience we kids enjoyed involved exploring a network of tunnels that existed in gorse vegetation and scrub bordering the edge of the Close. The tunnel's labyrinthine nature was a brilliant place to escape to, and a marvel and magnet for us kids. Moving along inside we crawled on our tummies using arms and elbows to drag us along forwards or backwards. We often surfaced and came out of an exit looking like commandoes, which of course we were in those minutes of play. Overactive imaginations ran rife in this maze and our ability to act any military role fitted the scene. Trying to lose a new recruit in the tunnels was a regular occurrence, especially if they had not known of the tunnels' existence till just before they entered them. What pains we must have been, leaving some poor, frightened child in that darkened area, cold, damp and alone, shouting for his mum. But then, that's how we all learned.

A more foolhardy way to a clobbering was to get caught at scrumping. Many was the time I returned home with bellyache from scoffing un-ripened apples, pears or plums from a nearby orchard and tried to explain to my parents that I wasn't hungry and didn't feel like eating the prepared meal. Most of this scrumping was always carried out under the guidance and presence of older kids. When I and my mates were eight or nine years old there would be some older twelve or thirteen year olds to pass on their skills and *modus operandi*. That was just the way it was: we'll teach you, you collect for us. However, my own career as a scrumper terminated when I was about 13 years old. I'd gone with some mates – I use the term lightly – and visited the senior hospital doctor's garden which had a lovely big orchard of mixed fruits that young pilferers adored to raid. There was I, up a tree having my desserts, when a voice from below startled me. It was the senior doctor himself and I'd been rumbled. With nowhere to hide, I had to concede defeat there and then in his fruit tree. As I climbed down he suggested that if I was hungry he would take me into his house and feed me any meal I could manage, so long as I had room in my stomach. OUCH! Did that have an effect on me, but even worse, I imagined he would tell my father who, on having been told of my crime, would then seek me out and give me a good thrashing. Well I received no thrashing for that misdemeanour on this occasion, and from that moment on, my career as a scrumper was over for good.

One time with friends that absolutely embarrassed me was the occasion when, at the age of about six years, I went swimming in a pool for the first time. Imagine my horror as I waited with my woollen trunks rolled up inside my towel waiting for my young mate to call for me. My mother opened the door when he knocked and said

"Make sure he doesn't get his hair wet!"

Can you ever imagine the total and utter humiliation I suffered then and there? For the rest of my life whenever I met up with those fellow swimmers I am reminded of her intervention. The look on their faces at that moment said it all, as their minds went into overtime thinking "She cannot be serious!" What an introduction to my career as a swimmer and in front of my mates too!

These same mates, believe it or not, the scrumpers, the tent dwellers and the swimmers earned a little legitimate money on the side as angelic choir boys. At a penny a choir practice, two-pence a service and a whole half-crown for a wedding they, and eventually me, put on collar, cassock and surplice three times on a Sunday and sang our hearts out. Sometimes we were in tune, but always sang our hearts out. The Eucharist, Matins and Evensong were fixtures in our monetary calendar for many years as we paraded like little Lord Fauntleroy's for the vicar, choirmaster and parents. But little did they know that following the Eucharist, the vicar would leave the church to partake of his breakfast. When he left the church some of the older choristers slipped into the vestry and then the sherry cupboard to sample its wares. When they were no longer paid for attending choir and left the choir, the next generation followed in their footsteps quite literally, and into the sherry cupboard. Need I say more? The sherry representing the blood of Christ must have been the most watered down on the planet, but amazingly nothing was ever said of this heinous crime by congregation or vicar! Further sacrilegious goings on were to be found in the belfry, when we could not access the sherry from the vestry. After the Eucharist and before Matins we were somehow allowed to ring the bells to call the converted to church. Well, that was the grand idea. Something went wrong along the way and the noise was far from musical, bringing the vicar back early from his breakfast, often chewing on his bacon. The sight he would have found was not as he would have wanted: choristers smoking, drinking who knows what, and several of us half way up the belfry tower hanging from the bell pulls. Not a pretty sight and one that was not often repeated, although years later, under supervision, we were given lessons in bell ringing, if we wanted them. Gone are the days but not the memories. Then there were the day trips from the church on the choir boys' outings to the seaside. These were often nightmarish and as memorable as a boil on your bum. We seemed to travel for most of the day just to get to the selected seaside resort and, if our luck was in, spend a couple of hours on the beach or on pleasure rides, followed by more hours on the coach travelling back home. This was not guaranteed to make me sing any better, nor was it my idea of fun. But our masters always meant well, I'm sure, as they bored us to death.

After the Evensong service on Sunday night, most of us trogged off to the church youth club to play table tennis, drink coffee and other 'things' in the dark at the back of the church hall. Life was never dull or boring for a youngster growing up at this time, and was loads of fun. At least, it was for me.

The Hospital

Living in Wilson Close I was never far away from the influence of the Pastures Hospital. This huge psychiatric unit of two thousand beds was home for many clients, thought to be mentally ill, from all over Derbyshire and occasionally further afield.

Both my parents worked there. My father worked through the ranks to become, before his retirement, Night Superintendent. My mother, a part-time nurse to begin with, picked up a career truncated by War and childbirth, and became a full time Ward Sister and finally, after re-training, a Clinical Tutor. I remember clearly, in 1960, my father returning home with his weekly pay packet to announce to my mother that he had just begun to earn £1000 a year. For him and us, at that time, a huge sum!

The hospital, to us three kids at number 14 Wilson Close, was all consuming: the houses belonged to the

Hey Teacher, You're 'aving a Larf

hospital; our parents belonged to the hospital by way of their jobs and we did, by way of our recreation and friendship groups. The only occasion we escaped the hospital's clutches was by attending church, shopping in the village at Mickleover, or in Derby, and of course, by attending school. Otherwise, we were utterly influenced by the Pastures Hospital. Not that that was in anyway detrimental, *au contraire*. We were entertained, often free of charge, by functions and events organised by the hospital on behalf of its clients, staff and staff families. Such was the range of activities to choose from it was easy to forget that the village of Mickleover was less than a mile away, or that the city of Derby was just three miles down the main road.

A keen young sportsman I could play cricket, football, tennis, bowls and, much later, golf. I could attend the 'flicks' every Thursday in the hospital theatre and watch a variety of westerns, comedies or thrillers. Of course, there was always a popular cartoon at the start of the evening's proceedings, but no ice-creams. We were able to attend Christmas parties where all the hospital staff's children received a substantial present from Father Xmas – I remember one year mine was that amazing and wonderful 'Magic Robot', a magnetic quiz game that bamboozled me for weeks, until I understood how it worked. We all attended the hospital Sport's Day on a summer Saturday and had the time of our lives. And, when much older, we were allowed to attend the dance that finished the Sport's Day off – and many staff too! Similarly, we attended the hospital New Year's Eve dance, legendary, not only for its dancing, but also for the alcohol consumed and the relationships that developed, or finished, on that evening of high spirits.

For me though, growing to like my sports as I did more and more, I became magnetised by the cricket and football played on the immaculate hospital sports field. My father played both sports too and we eventually played cricket together from 1959. On match days I would walk the three quarters of a mile to the ground from home, following my father who had cycled to the cricket field earlier, or he went there straight from work. For me, watching the game and operating the medieval scoreboard was a joy, not only because I knew all the players, but because I had a free cricket tea, the like of which was unavailable elsewhere. They were just brilliant. Sandwiches with ham, cheese or paste were supplemented by fantastic, huge jam tarts, Swiss rolls, fruit cake to die for, and the strongest cup of tea in all England. 'Of all the teas in all the world ......'

The cricket team included nursing staff and doctors, and also their relations. That was how I got my big chance to play cricket for them when I was ten years old. After 6 o'clock on match days, one of the players, who served in the Royal Air Force as a pilot, had to return to base, and I was always asked to field as his substitute. Did I need asking twice? Not a chance. As my own skill at the sport developed, not only was I eventually asked to play for the cricket team when I was twelve, but was soon bowling at men. After further coaching I opened the bowling at fourteen with my father, then forty-two - something he never stopped telling people, particularly after I was forty! I remember, when I was seventeen, breaking a batsman's arm and the next batsman refused to come to the wicket to bat because, he said, I was bowling too fast. Nothing wrong with the pitch in those days either. Still, it was a good grounding for my cricket later in life. Incredibly, during my first year of teaching, I went home for the weekend and was asked to play for the hospital team. That August Bank Holiday was perhaps the most successful weekend's cricket of my life statistically. On that Saturday, Sunday and August Bank Holiday Monday in 1968, I scored 107, not out, which included 16 fours and 6 sixes, and took 8 wickets for 13 runs in the first game. I hit 88, not out, and had 6 wickets in the second game on the Sunday, and finally, 56, not out, and 7 wickets in the last game. The most successful weekend of my life cricket-wise? You bet! Perhaps that early practice paid off. If only that weekend's luck could have reoccurred more often in my playing career.

Cricket and tennis occupied most of my time, with friends, in the school summer holidays, practising in the cricket nets or on the hard tennis courts. Those idyllic days were only ever spoiled by the weather, and kept us occupied, off the streets and out of trouble. In winter, football ruled, and after playing for school on a Saturday morning, from the age of eighteen, I turned out for the hospital team at centre forward in the afternoon. The year before, I had played for a successful under-seventeen youth team at the British Legion in Mickleover and, if I had not smoked cigarettes then, who knows what might have been? With the hospital team we travelled all over Derbyshire and Staffordshire in local leagues, sometimes successfully, sometimes miserably. Having played on some of the colliery pitches in North Derbyshire, I reckon I know good mud when I see it: sometimes ankle-high, it was impossible to play football on. Slip-sliding yes, but not football. At the same time, through my school team, I had become a regular player in the Derbyshire County Grammar Schools side and in a bad winter, pitch-wise, in 1963, even managed to arrange a County game at Pastures Hospital against Staffordshire.

Sport for me and my school friends was a large part of our lives, so when introduced to the supposed sedentary pastime of bowls, we took to it like ducks to water. The bowling greens were in excellent condition at the hospital, and were available for patients and staff to play on. With regular fixtures at weekends and midweek, all part of a hectic calendar, watching the ruthlessness with which the games were played, increased not only our knowledge of the game, but gave us a good insight into the characters that played the game. Many of the male staff who had played cricket and soccer graduated to become bowlers, often taking along their wives. Several staff became county bowlers. My mother, Doris, much later in her life, played for both Staffordshire and Derbyshire. Now though, in the 1950's the children of hospital staff would visit the bowling greens, sit on the vast grassy banks watching a game of bowls in progress whilst the sun shone, and for them, it must have been heaven. The tennis courts, too, were available both for staff and their families, and I can still see and hear my sister, Helen, walloping her friends on court even now. There were tarmac courts, or the surface preferred by me and my friends, a sort of *red gras*, on a secluded court at the back of the admissions ward, which became our Wimbledon. Hours of sets played, no line judges present and cheating was out of control as we played our Wimbledon matches daily, in season. Who could win with such flagrant disregard of the rules? It's about the same down Wimbledon way now isn't it? Chris Delve and I never agreed close line calls and had to play those points again. It's a wonder we ever finished a set.

Whatever the recreational aims of the Health Authority were when they set up the hospital, seeing all the sporting facilities in use on a summer's day and the participation by patients and staff alike, must have been just what the doctors ordered. The tiered banking allowed spectators to watch any of the particular sports in progress, and enabled patients/clients to be brought out to watch from the wards - surely all part of their rehabilitation.

The community element was all too evident at this time, principally based around sport, but encroaching into other areas too. One other important day on the hospital calendar was the annual Sport's Day. Chiefly for staff and patients, this magical day also involved families and children. Stalls sold goods of all kinds, while games and other amusements were spread all over the sports field. Pillow fighting, on a purpose-built stand, helped make the whole day come alive competitively. Just looking forward to going to the sport's day, to watch, was exciting enough for the youngster. Perhaps it might not be allowed nowadays though with the 'PC' brigade around because of the .... enjoyment? How do people find entertainment in this day and age? The stalls included cake stalls, coconut shies, but Tanks - a game that involved rolling an oval and weighted wooden block down a slope between gaps to get a prize- was definitely my favourite. There were also Lucky number ticket stalls for more adult prizes of booze or chocolates; bottle stalls of all kinds, Aunt Sally (knocking down tins from a shelf with tennis balls) and many I've forgotten, which all made up this wide variety of thrilling stalls and fun. The running races, whether for children, patients or staff, all had super prizes for the winners. Sack races, three-legged races, running races and egg-and-spoon races for boys or girls, males or females, all combined to provide a level of entertainment and fun so often missing nowadays. Throwing the cricket ball often provided shocks, in that non- cricketers often won the top prize! The tug- of- war raised tensions and blood pressure, but again, provided amusement. The climax to all the events was always the pillow fighting. Refereed competently, with the safety of large mattresses under the combatants, competitors would sit, cross–legged, on a horizontal pole above the ground and proceed, with specially designed pillows, to knock seven bells out of each other. The challenge was all too easy to become involved in: all the macho blokes, staff and patients and sometimes ladies, would line up to have a crack at someone on this activity. You can only imagine the roar of approval when the favourite on the pole lost his or her bout and the cacophony of noise if a patient beat a member of staff. The day was rounded off in the hospital theatre and dance hall where an Awards Evening completed the day's proceedings. The bar was often the winner at the end of the day, but the community had come together, once more, and was safe in its own boundaries as usual.

Whilst growing up in this safe environment, I came to know some patients by their first names, talking to them as the situation allowed, often about sport. When I returned home from college, unable to find temporary holiday employment on a building site, a hospital job as a temporary nursing assistant would always fill the gap. Throughout my three year college course I was able to work during my Xmas and Easter holidays at the hospital and thoroughly enjoyed, and gained by the experience. I was variously pushed into and locked inside a padded cell by 'friends'; I passed out at the sight of a patient being administered ECT (electroconvulsive therapy) when I should have been caring for him; and in the male geriatric unit, Woodlands, I saw and dealt with my first, but by no means my last, dead body. My first dead body experience in the geriatric unit concerned a lovely gentleman named Frank Eaton. His name is still indelibly etched in my mind. He died of cancer one night after a long and painful illness, right in front of me. I had been talking to him the evening before, and the night he died, although he was so ill and in pain, he never complained. Frank was a wonderful chap. I lit the joss sticks to help ameliorate the smell around his bed, and when I suspected he had died, I checked it out by placing a small, steel pocket mirror under his nostrils, to see if any condensation appeared on it from his breathing. James Bond had copied me and my method in a recent film that year! The cleaning of the body, and the sealing of all orifices, was altogether another experience the reader could well do without me expanding on here. Whilst I worked there, another patient in Woodlands, whose name springs to mind, is that of Freddie Parkinson. A seventy-five year old patient at the time, he had been hospitalised as a three year old! His crime or psychiatric condition you ask? Wetting the bed! This was now Xmas 1964 and Freddie had been in institutions since 1892. When I heard that he had been in hospitals for so long, I just could not comprehend the tragedy of it all. It got worse too. He was able to recall the date that EVERY member of staff, that he had come into contact with, had started at the hospital; those who went to war and who returned and those who started, like me, as a temporary assistant, and each and every time I returned. He was a fascinating man, clean, well dressed and a pleasure to talk to. I just could not believe that he had suffered this fate for so long.

Working in Woodlands was a superb experience, enhanced by members of staff who were often larger than life itself, and with humour to match. Three stood out for me: Albert Lilley, Jack Pegg and Ivan Harewood. Albert was my mate's dad and the charge nurse in command of the unit. He had received a war medal of the highest order for helping to nurse Sir Winston Churchill back to health, during the war, after 'Winnie' had suffered a bout of pneumonia. Jack Pegg was the unit's chef. Ivan Harewood was a highly trained nurse and the first Afro-Caribbean I had talked with about racism. I was in total awe of his presence. All were to play an important role in my life from the moment I met them. Albert, whose sense of humour was legendary, was a good nurse who knew his stuff and knew the

Hey Teacher, You're 'aving a Larf

patients, treating them with respect and humouring them as and when. He taught me a great deal about humility and how to treat people who needed caring for. Jack cooked the most amazing breakfasts which we all ate sitting down together, after the patients had been finished theirs, and because the meals were so huge, we probably could have gone to sleep afterwards. Ivan was just one of the most impressive people I have ever met. I met him years later in his Barbados Church, and when his procession stopped at my seat we shook hands, hugged each other, and tears in our eyes freely flowed. No wonder that working casually in Woodlands was one of the happiest times of my life. Maybe it was because of all the snooker I played during the quieter times on the ward or the early finishes when Albert allowed me to leave my shift early to go and play football for the hospital team. All made this happy time of my life that much more pleasant.

Around this time of Sixth Form and College education, I was hanging out with a good friend who also lived near to the hospital, the third son of the hospital bailiff, Jimmy Hirst. He had two brothers, John and Richard who were in the Canadian Mounties and my visits to the Hirst's hospital farm often involved me being regaled at length, by his mother, about life in Canada and the Mounties in particular. This was a hell of a strain on Jim, poor sod! Nevertheless, little did his parents know that we schemed to use the family's snooker table most Saturdays, when mum and dad were out, and Jim was able to educate me about the importance of whisky and gin! Many were the times I had to cycle home late, on a Saturday night, under the influence of alcohol, up the steep hill leading from the farm to the major road that would take me homewards. Then, cycling that final mile, getting off the bike, opening the door to try and pretend, whilst leaning against the settee in the living room, that we'd had 'shush' a good time playing 'ssshhhnooker' all night! Jim taught me to drive a car, at the age of fourteen, around the hospital grounds. Well, not a car exactly. I should say in, or on, the chassis of an old Ford Popular. It was bloody dangerous at corners, even when corners did not exist! He also taught me how to use a shotgun properly as we often went looking in the barns at the farm for vermin to shoot. Growing up at that time was never dull, as I keep saying, but I wonder whether it could be the same today for boys like me. I don't think so.

Two student nurses at the hospital that I played cricket and football with were John Lander and Cliff Thompson. When I was seventeen they invited me to go on holiday with them to Skegness and stay in the Lander's family caravan. I'm easily conned and believed it would be similar to one of those fantastic caravans seen in the American trailer parks, in films. I should have been so lucky! Having taken the bus from Derby to Skegness, and been stuck on it most of that first Saturday of the holiday, and being excited at what was about to be laid out before us in terms of luxury caravanning, it came as a shock, that night, to be spending a week in the wettest, mouldiest, most uninhabitable and coldest caravan on earth. Some holiday that was. Not only was the caravan a health hazard, but it rained all the damned holiday week too!!

Primary School and the Start of Formal Education

Mickleover County Primary School, the village school, was a mile from where we lived in Wilson Close and was where I started my formal education in 1950. Seems a long time ago now, and in those early days I was in Mrs Ravensdale's class, stationed in a desk at the front. Can't think why, but I hadn't been there long before I was in trouble. Not, I may add, for any educational problem although there were plenty, but for urinating down Martin Buck's neck! I received two strokes of the cane on my left hand, and I had to wear a yellow dunce's hat from morning break through to lunch time.

Such an injustice should never have occurred in the first place. From my point of view, I was ensconced and in place at the toilet – a contraption that was "open air" and with a wall just above head height front and back, with a gutter on the ground leading to a drain which took the 'liquid' away. Anyway, the toilet always stank and there we boys were, trying to see who could pee the highest and if possible over the wall, when into the toilet came Martin Buck, my next door neighbour at Wilson Close. He was a whole three and a half months older than me and in a higher class and knew well the school procedures as he had started school the previous term. What he did not know, at that very precise moment, as he spun me round on my heels and tried to take my place in the toilet, was that I was still peeing in the air. This pee should have fallen back to earth as my aim was still vertical but down it came on poor Martin's head and clothes. He screamed and ran out of the toilet. To this day I have little recollection of him beginning to pee, but I know he reported me, which is how I came to take my punishment. I must have been the youngest in the school to be caned as I'd only been there a few weeks. Martin only ever toileted alongside me after that, even when we had grown up and were mates. Can't think why!

Such an inauspicious beginning could not last, could it? I seemed to be watched very closely by staff after that, especially at break times in case my notoriety turned into a habit I guess. The teachers need not have bothered because as soon as the break-times began I was out in the playground playing football or cricket until we had to line up in an orderly queue before going to

Hey Teacher, You're 'aving a Larf

eat our dinner in the hall. Soon, in class, I was being told off for misshaping my letters in my alphabet and numbers book, and my writing looked as though I had used a broken stick to write with. And could I write my sentences on the lines in the book? Of course this was not true was it? Oh yes it was, so they kept me in at morning break on many an occasion, for 'extra practice' I think they called it. If only they had allowed me to write with my left hand like I desperately wanted to! Mrs Ravensdale was not my favourite teacher and she was the first school teacher I experienced, damn it. I was so glad, eventually, to be 'promoted' to Infant class Two - Mrs Wibberley's class. After my First Year experiences with Mrs Ravensdale, who was a bloody monster to me, the next year would be a piece of cake, wouldn't it? You see I had missed my favoured football games in the playground at break because I had to stay in her class, learning to write on lines in my books. So I quickly learnt to write on the lines in my books, because no way was I going to stay in Mrs Ravensdale's class.

Mrs Wibberley-Wobberley, as we called her, used to read to us and make us read to her and the whole class. In so doing created in all of us, and me in particular, the thirst to read 'proper' books. The joy of her activating my imagination through books was electric, even if I did fall asleep occasionally on a sunny summer day or a warm winter's afternoon. Then, all too soon I was on my way again to Mrs Hinchcliffe's class and the pace of education stepped up progressively. We all, each day, had to read to her and queue to have our 'sums' checked. We regurgitated our maths tables and we studied nature, or more to the point, painted and drew tree leaves. We began to find places on maps and learn some basic Geography, and of course, we began to read about days gone by in a subject that she called History.

At this top end of the Infant school we were allowed, if we wanted, to be extras in the school play or pantomime. We also were allowed to go around the school as milk monitors delivering crates of milk to other classes, and when it was my turn, did I give Mrs Ravensdale's class a wide berth.

Miss Wedd was the senior teacher in the Infant school and, as the day approached, when we entered her classroom, it was as if this was the judgement day of our lives that far. This was to be our first experience of what a battle-axe was really like! A woman, who by her very presence could crisp bacon, I was sure, by just looking at a rasher. A woman who could reduce you to a shivering, snivelling wreck just by greeting you in the morning as you arrived in her classroom as she bellowed her 'Good morning class.' A woman who would make you work till your wrist ached with writing, your eyes were sore with reading, and last but not least, she destroyed your whole macho image as you pranced, sorry danced, around the school hall to BBC Music and Movement as you 'fell like a leaf from a tree' or 'flew like a little sparrow home to its nest'!!!! A woman who should have been cloned and put in every school's classrooms today: there would be no problem with reading, writing and arithmetic under her considerable wing.

Moving on, the Xmas parties at the school were absolutely magical for us young kids: the decorations we had made, the hall we prepared, the food we could smell – jellies and trifles in wax containers with cherries and angelica, cake, sandwiches with salmon paste, meat paste, any paste just because it was Xmas. Crackers, the tree with decorations, the crib with the baby Jesus and of course the present we each received at the end of the night from Santa Claus. Not forgetting the gift of chocolate bars, fruit gums or pastilles from the proprietor, across the road from school, Oliver and Winspear that topped off the whole night. We nearly always, at this age, skipped home, as we were so full of Xmas cheer. The crescendo of expectation and excitement that was building up to this party day was incredible and had to be experienced, as only a child could. We were ready to burst with anticipation. Every day, from then on, became Xmas day until the day itself came and …… went all too quickly.

Moving up into the Junior School was relatively smooth and without any problems for most children, including me. This was probably because the two schools shared the same site, playgrounds, and routines, and pupils were 'well known' to the Junior School staff. I was to find myself travelling, educationally, a year in front of where I should have been. I have no idea why I was in Standard One at seven years of age and didn't bargain for having two years in Standard Four, the top class, in times to come. At seven years old I didn't care either and for me, the romance of school and all it entailed was just like a fairy story. I simply adored school and couldn't wait to leave home early in the morning to get there, and as I grew older that time got much earlier. So much so that in the summer I often ran the mile to school all the way without stopping, either to get the cricket bat if I arrived first before 7.30am, or the cricket ball if I was second to arrive behind 'Stoffer' Gascoigne.

In the classroom whether chanting tables in 'sums', reading aloud in English, learning about Tupik the Eskimo in Geography or reading 'March of Time' Book One about Romans in History, the whole time just passed by too quickly for me. The really hard work for me was handwriting with those pens with the silly, replaceable nibs. I say this because I was forced to write with my right hand, not the left, which for me was more natural. Much later, when I taught in the classroom, I was able to write on the blackboard with either hand, sometimes, according to my pupils, better with my left hand! My handwriting to this day leaves much to be desired. Anyway, that was not the fault of my teacher, Mr Roscoe, an absolute giant of a man who encouraged me to try potato-printing instead, a subtle try sir, but again with very little success. He also encouraged my football skills in winter, despite my mother's attempts to make me look as though I had Dixie Dean's shorts on. Dixie was a famous Everton and England footballer in the Thirties and the fashion in those days was very, very long shorts, if you get my drift! Did I look a fool in those shorts?

But, as in my History books, time marches on, and the following year in Standard Two my teacher was Miss Plumpton. For me, she was just like the old battleaxe, Miss Wedd, in the Infants: she made me do extra handwriting and go through my letters of the alphabet with those awful pens. The alphabet I knew, but the pens, aargh! I must have kept the blotting

Hey Teacher, You're 'aving a Larf

paper manufacturers in business that year: so many blots, so much mess, so much 'repeat that again until it is done properly'. If she hadn't relented I'd still be there now probably, which is why my writing is still a mess. But the good thing was that I knew my tables and was really good at spelling and with antonyms and synonyms I'll have you know. I thought I was a proper little star. It was around this time in the class that my mates and I started to sound more like snakes the amount of hissing we did to 'Miss!' as we put our hands up, with or without the correct answers. It was also the first time I had been in such a large class of about forty plus pupils, and met this pupil, who, when he 'hissed' to 'Miss', always forgot the answer when she asked him for it. Lord knows what he has done since those days, job-wise.

In the November of that school year, 1952, I was rushed into hospital to have my appendix taken out, but failed to have the operation because I also had pneumonia and it was deemed to be too dangerous to operate. However, it was whilst in this class that I started to play serious football for the school team, aged seven. Playing with older pupils especially 'Soss' Hulland and Allan Bradshaw was some experience, believe me, and stood me in good stead for later years. The school outing that year, 1953, was to the Blue John Mines near Castleton, North Derbyshire where once off the hired coach we scratched around everywhere on the floor looking for the precious Blue John stone. Coincidentally, it was the year we all had to draw pictures of the new queen, Queen Elizabeth the Second, and since her coronation was on second of

June, 1953, we all had the day off school. The mug we received looked excellent at first, especially with NHS orange juice in it for a few days, and then the gold print wore off the side of the glass mug!

In Standard Three the teacher was a Mr Peach and he became the first male teacher I was to see get angry. When he did, and it was not often, he seemed to blow his cheeks out, go very red and shout so loud he could have woken up the dead! But despite this, I loved his lessons and began to take a far greater interest in cricket and football, playing for the school and travelling even further afield to play the fixtures. The manager of the football team was the Deputy Head and Standard Four teacher, Mr Bagley, and he encouraged me to play up front in the team, on the left wing. I think this was primarily because I was the only player to kick well with both feet.

Lunch times in school were always a laugh for me because these two male teachers, Mr Bagley and Mr Peach, invariably sat together. Nothing wrong in that, I hear you say, but they ate so differently which caused us kids to stare in amazement towards them. Mr Peach, the taller of the two moved his jaws so quickly when eating rather mouse-like, chomping away like an express train, that you would think he had to grease his jaws each night to stop them from seizing up! Mr Bagley meanwhile, chewed so sedately and much slower and looked to be taking such an age it always seemed possible he would never finish his meal. The remarkable thing was, for the young observer, that they both seemed to swallow their food at the same time and their plates were always emptied at the same time.

Hey Teacher, You're 'aving a Larf

The mimics amongst us had a field day, until we espied the two men appearing to watch us. At that moment we young people watchers dropped our heads to avoid their stares, the teachers obviously wondering what we were so animated about, and finished our meal quickly before we slunk off back to the playground.

Finally, the school trip that year was to Liverpool, and amongst the main sights we saw was the now defunct Liverpool Overhead Railway. All those kids manically pressing their noses against the carriage windows: thank God for Kleenex!

Time was flying by really quickly now and with so much to do in and out of school, in the classroom and on the games field. A year early I joined Standard Four but not with Mr Bagley, who had left to teach in South Staffordshire, but with the new Deputy Head, Mr Gaskell. He had taught in a large Derby School who were our greatest rivals on the football field, Alveston and Boulton. For two years I had this young teacher and in my final year of the 11+ examination, his bearing and influence on my future was critical.

The final two years at Junior School were for me again were absolutely magical. The classroom was a stage: the lessons taught and the skills and knowledge acquired and learnt all seemed to click into place in those two years. Maybe the exercise I was getting, through all the sporting activities I undertook, stimulated my brain. The football was coming on a treat and for school I was scoring goals from all over the park: for the Trent Valley District side I was scoring from the left wing, and both my mother and Nan came to the games to watch me play! In one game for school against Little

Eaton School, I distinctly remember shooting the ball from just outside my own penalty box, down a slope and with the wind behind, hit it over the goalie's head at the other end and into the net *a la Beckham*. As I write this, and if he ever reads the book, Mr Gaskell who is still alive I know, would remember that goal I'm sure. At cricket, my favourite sport at the time, I had to either cut my run-up down to almost 'no yards' or bowl at half pace in the games lessons because no-one wanted to bat against this demon bowler, aged ten!

Pity that all this enthusiasm and success nearly exploded in my face at the time of the 11+. I had not realised, or been partial too, any bad blood between me or my family and the Head Teacher at the time, Mr Best. I say this because during the school examinations, tests and 11+ practice papers in the last two years my results were as good, if not better, than 95% of the class. That is not a boast, it was just the way we were 'trained' and coached towards the examination. Therefore parents' evenings for my mum were a joy as she sat and listened to Mr Gaskell saying the good and the bad. I'm convinced her ears were only tuned into the bad though: 'He says you balance on two chair legs' or 'You still hiss when you put your hand up to answer a question' and lastly, 'He says you always want to go to the toilet when you come in from break or dinnertime'. But after the last parents' evening prior to me taking and sitting the 11+, something was not quite right. From what she said to my father that night after the school meeting things appeared to have gone pear-shaped and I would not get to grammar school. All my efforts were to be

Hey Teacher, You're 'aving a Larf

for nothing if Mr Best had his way and I did not get a place at the grammar school.

Now that upset my mum when she was told the news by Mr Gaskell and she took it upon herself to go and see Mr Best the headmaster. It was not a good idea to upset Doris and let other pupils with lesser IQ<u>s</u> than her little Lawrence, even though he was a ragged-arsed ranger, go to grammar school and she was not to be beaten. (Just who was taking this exam?) The upshot of all this was that Mr Gaskell bore down on me like a ton of bricks, making me work even harder in class: my mother purchased extra intelligence books from WH Smith's bookshop in Derby and I had to practise these bloody tests every night and more. Failure was now out of the question.

So on the big day of the tests, and the usual questions from parents afterwards as to how we'd got on, the only way I could escape this pressure was to spend time on my sports. On the day the 11+ result's letter came into school, we pupils had to address the envelope for Mr Gaskell to place the results letter in. On the way home I remember my mates and I skipped most of the way playing tag, and not the least bit interested in getting home to open the important letter. That was until I dropped my letter in the road and some thoughtless bus driver ran over it leaving a very large tread mark all over the envelope! Picking the envelope out of the gutter, I could, at that very moment, feel the clip behind my ear from either or both my parents. So once at home I did get my ear clipped for dropping the envelope, followed by some big cuddles as my mother screamed at me, from no yards, that I had passed to go to grammar school. What an emotional turn-around in the space of a micro-second.

The school trip to London for me later that year came and went, I was so disinterested. After all, I had been there the previous year, seen all the sights, done all the museums, got the posters and written up my 'school trip experiences to our capital city' last year. I again sat on my tomato and cheese sandwiches crushing them and warming them, cracked and eaten my hard boiled egg, and finished off my picnic as I swigged my NHS orange juice from its corked bottle. How was I to be excited? By the train we travelled on of course. Steam trains; express steam trains from Derby Midland to St Pancras, the life blood of the nation. The big steel monsters travelled very fast to the capital city hauling, as part of its cargo, over sixty excited youngsters that were about to leave junior school for pastures new in only a few weeks' time. All I remember after that last trip at school was the leaving ceremony and the presentation of prizes on the last day. I was fortunate to receive the sports prize for that year, 1957, a cricket bat that I was to treasure for years. I remember going into the sports shop and thanking the proprietor for the bat days later, I was so chuffed. But, on that last day, as with other last days at school for other pupils, the final hymn was always 'Lord, dismiss us with thy blessing, thanks for mercies past received…..'

We sang that hymn at the top of our little voices, the whole school getting louder as we progressed up the years, not so much because we liked it but because we were just about to start 5 weeks summer holiday! Ha! Ha! Bloody Ha!

Secondary Education

Having left the Junior School my education was supposed to continue at John Port co-educational Grammar School, Etwall, a brand new school in south Derbyshire that had started life in 1956 with a Third Year and a First Year intake. With such newness came a young, vibrant and enthusiastic staff, with experienced senior teachers who were to lead the way. This was my educational home from 1957 to 1964 and as such gave me some of my life's happiest memories, educationally, sports-wise and socially.

To begin, there were three fundamental changes from the previous school: we travelled by bus the three miles to the school, complete with free bus pass; we wore an ugly uniform which included pale blue peaked caps; and we changed lessons and teachers when the bell rang. My heavy school satchel was always full of blue jotters, dark blue maths books, green English books, orangey Geography books, grey Physics books etc, etc. Far too much to hump around for us youngsters, but woe betide anyone who forgot their exercise book for said subject! On top of this heavy hoard of books, we had PE kit to carry around each lesson for when we were in the gym, on the playing fields or on the tennis courts. This helped the shoulders grow wider and biceps stronger. That's my story, anyway.

A daily assembly ritual began the school day in the School Hall first thing in the morning with a hymn and lesson read from the lectern. This ritual usually contained a Bible-reading by staff and later by pupils as the school grew in size. That was the order each and every day for all the assemblies I attended at this school. The school assembly was the medium chosen to set the disciplinary standards for the day too, where school rules were reinforced, the law laid down and where the lawbreakers were brought to book. Not only were school notices and results given out, but also a roll-call of the 'fallen' pupils. After the assembly these pupils would be seen waiting outside the Head's office expecting to be punished. Pupils rarely went there to be praised, only to be punished. That's how it seemed to the younger pupils because all the praise for teamwork, or educational achievement, had been dealt with in the assembly. However, God help anyone caught twitching their face, or moving a muscle, whilst the assembly was in progress. If some poor soul sang out of tune, or had a genuine coughing fit and smirked nervously because of it, that meant trouble too, so we often mimed the words to the hymns and tried desperately to stifle any sudden coughs. Worse still, knowing that you had transgressed, came that awful fear of breaking wind accompanied by the necessary fidgeting, trying to deny ownership of the methane! I bet even the staff felt guilty and went red-faced when Mr. Payne, the Head teacher, gave a whole-school rollicking in those days.

Once 'free' to go to lessons, further military discipline encroached on our lives. We moved on the left hand side only when going down corridors or upstairs, and we stood in straight lines outside classrooms, boys on this side, girls the other side. Whilst lining up we had to stare at the back of the head of the person in front - not easy if he was four foot nothing and you were six foot plus. We were not allowed to talk in those lines and if we did, a ton of bricks came down on us so to speak in the form of detentions, lines, or worst of all we were made to stand outside the classroom, alone. That was a mortal sin, and if the Head came past when you were outside the classroom, he would always ask why you were standing there. If you were not convincing enough with your answer then you might well be whisked off to his 'caning emporium' (I knew he had a wide selection of canes) and summarily dealt with. It is probably relevant now to tell of the two times I had the cane from the Head, and why. The first time I was caned, I genuinely have no idea what my three friends and I had done wrong. Seriously! Typical of fifteen year-olds I suppose. There we were waiting in the rain, outside the Art room in the corridor, which we later were to find out was the crime: wrong place, wrong time! The Head, unseen by us, was on the prowl that lunch time with one of his canes in his hand. When he saw us, from a distance in the Art room corridor, his eyes positively bulged with 'disciplinary anticipation'. (i.e. He felt a caning in the wind!) Charging down the steps from the staffroom he had us trapped: if we left the Art room area he would have seen us anyway so we just stood still, and, like rabbits in the glare of headlights, we froze to the spot, giggled nervously as you do in those circumstances of abject fear, and I'm sure we nearly peed ourselves. More wind, Headmaster? He flew into the passageway, then into the main art room and proceeded to throw fairly large tables across the Art room floor with one hand, like a man possessed of amazing strength, creating space for him to wield his trusty cane. We had to bend over one of those tables, now in disarray, and he then gave each of us four strokes of the cane on our backsides whilst appearing to hold his breath all the time that he thrashed us. I don't think I have ever seen, before or since, an adult's face change colour, or contort so much as his face did in those few moments. He could have been Lon Chaney's double! Afterwards, when he had done his deed, we had to leave the Art room area quickly and head back to where we should have been in the first place. It is no fun when your pants and backside are on fire I can tell you. The other guys, you ask, what are they doing now? One became a senior social worker; another a senior member of the Canadian Mounted Police Force; and the last made a fortune in computers from some London authority. The GLC rings a bell. Did the caning serve a purpose? Definitely not because not long after two of us were in trouble again.

This time I can tell you the date of the offence as it is forever etched in my mind: May 5th 1961. How

Hey Teacher, You're 'aving a Larf

do I know? Because it was the day Commander Alan Sheppard became the second man in space in a module called Freedom 7. What was our crime this time? We had, sadly, become trapped in the toilets adjacent to the classroom where we were due to have a Physics lesson with a new and young lady teacher. Of course the fact that someone just happened to have removed the door handle on the inside of the toilet so we had no way of getting out, didn't help matters. Furthermore, in an attempt to disturb our classmates and make them laugh or giggle, we wrote 'desperate messages' on toilet paper as only hostages to toilet humour can. Those international words 'HELP' and 'S.O.S.' were the ones and we hung them out of the toilet window so that all our class could see, and maybe help us in our hour of need. We thought we were being really original as we laughed and joked the lesson time away. Imagine our surprise when the Head appeared at the toilet's door having opened the door from the outside and bade us follow him, once again, to his 'caning emporium'. And we got off the charge! Hooray! That was because the Head softened, after listening to our tale of woe, on such an important day in history. God Bless America! In our classroom, after registration that afternoon, we were laughing our heads off behind our desk lids thinking we had escaped any punishment. All of a sudden there was a whoosh of rapidly moving feet, getting louder as they approached our desks. When my mate's head crashed to the bottom of his desk having had the lid slammed and closed very quickly on him, I instantly knew all was lost. We must have both gone white with shock, for there was the Head again screaming at the top of his voice,

"Told me a pack of lies you did! Follow me!"

And we knew where we were off to again! You know at that point, that the game is up and you're nicked. Even so, the nervous twitching of your eyes and mouth, the higher pitched voices that accompany fear and the giggling, cannot be subdued. The end was nigh as we struggled to keep up with the marching speed of the Head. We were given four more strokes of the cane on our backsides and I'm utterly convinced that, when I had a bath at home later that night, my bottom heated up the bath water! I could not sit down to eat either which must have amused my parents for a start. BUT, after that incident, I never had the cane again. Came close, didn't get caught, probably should have, but did not. Thank the Lord, that Head left at the end of our Fourth Year, never to trouble us again. A new Head came to the school, having taught on the other side of Derby, and we hoped he would be more lenient when tested. We hoped.

I hope all my cynicism came out in the last few paragraphs as I really wanted to cleanse myself of any negatives that I, as a pupil at this school, had felt were present in my mind because there were so many golden days in that school for me. It was perhaps my escape from life at home I suspect, but it would take years to recall the fun and laughter that my friends and I had together or the daft scrapes we got into. Perhaps it is easier to separate study and sports to illustrate this point. Studies were not easy but, by and large, enjoyable. My favourite subjects were Geography, History and Biology - all of which I swallowed avidly - unlike Maths and

Physics, which seemed to devour me! Who, in their right mind, would want to play with letters in Maths? We did that in English, didn't we? When I had left junior school, my arithmetic skills were good: I knew my tables, could add, subtract, multiply and divide very quickly in my head and loved it. Now, in this new world, it was algebra, geometry, trigonometry and logarithms. I didn't need them then and I don't need them today. Do I? In Maths therefore with little or no arithmetic from the first year, I was a lost soul. The same happened in Physics too which was why I ended up with Physics and Chemistry as a combined O-level years later. Abstract, that's what they were to me, but it was not the fault of the teachers who were a great laugh. Maybe that was my problem, playing the class clown. In the end I just didn't understand and kept quiet until I grew older, became bored, and then I looked elsewhere for entertainment. This often got me into trouble with staff as me and my mates acted the fool. Some of the japes were amazing, but then again we suffered because of it, either by having the slipper, or by being kept in after school - thus being unable to play in any football or cricket matches for that evening after school. That was a real sod, but I soon learned my lesson after a couple of misses and calmed down somewhat after the fourth year.

A subject that didn't amuse me at all was metalwork. I spent all year, a whole year, when I was thirteen years of age, making a pin holder. How pathetic was that? Not the task, but that it took me a whole year, as I was so useless. No budding engineer me and over the next fifty years I have proved it over and over again. It was obvious from the start that I never had a clue about anything mechanical and that lack of understanding is still with me today. Again it took me six months in woodwork to make a mortise and tenon joint, and I must have used a whole tree for the purpose. It was still skew-whiff in the end, or should I say the middle? I'd have been far better off learning to cook cheese and potato pie with sliced tomato on top, just like my sisters were to make later. Still there were other subjects to dig into and, as I have said, Geography and History were two of my favourites.

In selling a subject well and thereby stimulating pupils' taste-buds of interest, ability, sound discipline and enthusiasm for the subject is what I believe good teaching is about. This was certainly true in my case as two unrelated teachers sharing the same name - 'Geography' Holmes and 'History' Holmes, both Yorkshire men, inspired me with their riveting lessons. I used to take atlases to bed to read, heaven forbid, to memorise mountains, capes, capitals, rivers, anything to impress. It was the same with History, memorising dates and events just for my own fun and pleasure. Pity I did not have the same enthusiasm for my weaker subjects.

We all have faults and perhaps my worst subject in school was French and boy did it show. Did it show? I tried very hard to learn the language, even bunking off school to the pictures to see Brigitte Bardot in Burton-on-Trent! It failed as a French exercise and only served to increase my interest in the opposite sex, so it had purpose I think, of a biological nature. French lessons were compulsory and so my purgatory was never over until the end of the fifth year, when I got a place in the Sixth Form. The teachers of French must have thought I was from another world as I tried to learn my verbs and translate English to French or vice versa, because it often did not look like French. Maybe Polish?

I fully understand with hindsight why I never made the top 'A' forms and remained, throughout school, in the 'B' grade, although there was another grade below that I could easily have fallen into from time to time. However, I did have a modicum of unexpected success in English, though it was not one of my favourite lessons, but it became my most successful subject in the 'O' level examinations quite by sheer fluke. For English Language I obtained a good grade, but, amazingly, I scored top marks in Literature and all because, on the morning of the exam, in the upstairs toilet at home, I learnt, parrot–fashion, Mark Antony's oration speech in 'Julius Caesar', and stayed long enough to memorise Matthew Arnold's 'Dover Beach' poem. Guess what happened, apart from the pins and needles? The first two questions in the exam were on those two topics. So I gained top grade for English Literature which was totally undeserved. It showed one of the futilities of examinations when one person can be so lucky. More deserving people, probably, were not so lucky, or didn't spend enough time in their toilets.

The results meant I could enter the 6th Form and spend two more years playing sport, something that would come to haunt me and be reflected later in my 'A' level results! History, Geography and Economics were to be my torture for those two years. I say torture, not in Geography or History, but mainly in Economics, which

I failed to grasp, until I started my teaching career years later, and had to pay my own bills. The discipline and effort needed for 'A' levels I don't think is needed for a degree course today, which was my problem. I did not work as hard as I should have with my 'A' levels. To prove that point I was playing tennis when I should have been in a History exam and that was not the right attitude. Indeed, before my 'O' levels, my Maths teacher was to write in a report:

'If Anthony's (they always called me bloody Anthony) games-field enthusiasm invaded the classroom, he would surely be a good pupil.'

Absolutely true and if only ....

Sport and its 'periphery' were beginning to take me away from my studies far too often. For 'periphery' read 'young ladies and the social scene' and that seemed to accelerate in the 6th form. The PE/Games set in school were all mates together as they grew up and stayed together throughout the 6th form. The camaraderie was good and when they could the girls supported the boys matches and vice versa. Many eventually qualified as teachers and several of them taught PE. Friends I had then, and played all manner of sport with, I see all too infrequently now. They include Chris Delve, John Sansom, Guy Hall, Allan Bradshaw, Rick Smith, Jonathan Kitchell, Eric Knight, Jim Neilly, Malcolm Jacobs and many more whose names I cannot recall. Chris was a close mate but, when we played in opposing teams, we hammered each other as if we were mortal enemies. John and I used to play table tennis in the kitchen of his house till all hours before I bade goodnight to his sister, Gill. Guy was the best goalkeeper I have seen and played with and a really good county and England schoolboy wicket keeper. Playing together in the County Football team was an experience we shared in 1963-64. Allan Bradshaw was school football captain in the year above me and we played dozens of games in the same side throughout our school-life. The only player who regularly called for the ball as it was kicked from the goalie's hands, soared miles into the air, and as the ball fell to earth, there underneath it was Allan Bradshaw. (Not plastic balls in those days!) Eric Knight was a superb wing-half and as two 'over age' players in the county cup final, 1962, were in the team that beat Ashbourne School 13-2 that day. I scored nine goals in that game and was helped enormously by Jimmy Neilly who claims he was so quick over the pitch's turf he crossed the ball from both wings for me to score! Rick Smith, Jonathan Kitchell and I spent hours in the school cricket nets bowling over after over prior to school cricket matches, with Jonathan joining me in the nets at the hospital in the holidays as we continued our practice. Malcolm Jacobs and I were not only mates in school but we also spent six long weeks working at Butlin's Skegness 'learning the ropes' before we went to college. 1964 was an important year for the First XI football team as we beat Repton School 4-2 a major highlight for us grammar school boys, just as being thrashed at cricket by their prep' school, when we were in our second year, was a low point. Well we were all dismissed twice for about 41 runs, (that is in two innings) when they could only muster 180+, in their one innings. We were a sick bunch of thirteen year old cricketers that Saturday afternoon!

The social scene was becoming too active at this time of development for a young male. Young ladies were becoming a big distraction, for all the right reasons of course, and although it was not quite Cider with Rosie it was more like Lager with ……..well, you know.

Our group of young lady friends included in no particular order, Gill Sansom, Kay Hallam, Sally le Page, Cazzy Grimes, Joan Chambers, Gill Hall, Sheila Wilkins and Gill Allsebrook. During the school lunch-time we friends would often all collect on a sunny day, sit on the bank that overlooked the tennis courts, and watch others playing tennis or netball or listening to ………... Worker's Playtime of course starring Bernard Herman and the NDO or Vince Hill etc. Were we 'anoraks', 'dinosaurs', 'sad people' or what?

I said I have fabulous memories of this school, but some were strange and stand out more than others. One is of me and a group of friends who, as young 14 year old voyeurs, stood watching the Secondary School playground, which was two hundred yards away, opposite our gym. That day, and every day apparently, a young lady pupil was being 'serviced' by a succession of youths. She always had a queue whatever the weather, and, according to gossip never tired!

Another vivid memory is of my first and only trip to Malham in Yorkshire with the school, on a Geography field-trip. This put the physical Geography work we had already completed in class, into perspective, and related it to the 'field'. It was a tipping point for me and was to stimulate an interest that has stayed with me to this day playing a large influence on my own career.

Hey Teacher, You're 'aving a Larf

The third memory is of a fieldtrip to Barmouth in the 6th form with Chris Delve, Derek Hillyer and our Geography teacher Mr. Murdin who took us there in his little and green Morris Minor van. The scenery around Cader Idris was spectacular, and although, when we walked slowly up the mountain in misty, icy conditions, (it was Easter after all), Derek was to travel back down the mountain rather rapidly having slipped on some ice. About 400 yards in all! He was very lucky not to get seriously injured in those conditions, and having limped back to our waiting schoolteacher and his van was, because of his dented pride allowed to sit in the front seat all the way home!

The last memory in this batch concerns a fantastic trip to Whitehall Lodge, Buxton, an outdoor field and outward bound centre in north Derbyshire. The trip was the brainchild of our new headmaster, Mr P.K.Holl. The two weeks that we had there were fantastic: rock-climbing, mountain walking, pot-holing and just getting to know each other were part of the activities. There we were on that course in October 1963, in a cave several hundred feet underground for the majority of the Cuban crisis. Surfacing, we became aware that we could have all been blown to smithereens and not known why. We only found out as we paused for breath in a pub afterwards, of course, as Joe Brown nicked our fags. Our guides and leaders on that course were/are legends in the mountaineering sphere even today: Eric Langmuir was head warden; Joe Brown his deputy; and a gent named Mansell, who had been on an expedition to Mount Ararat, looking for Noah's Ark, I think, in 1961, made up three of the staff at the Lodge. Other names I have forgotten, but I have never forgotten the times we shared there as a group of young people, nor the pranks we got up to, at the expense of each other in a fortnight of learning without 'A' Level work.

In my final year I applied to P.E. colleges in expectation of becoming a Physical Education teacher. My interview at Loughborough fizzled out when Mr Stamatakis told me he wanted gymnasts, not games players. I thought that poppycock but my forecast 'A' level results were probably not what he wanted, or expected them to be, I suspected, if I was honest! He was right of course and that is why I went to St Peter's College, Saltley, in Birmingham, never regretted a moment, had a whale of a time, met loads of friends and did some work too.

Sad to say the only time I returned to John Port School, apart from visiting Geography Holmes one year, was to collect the PJ Wood trophy for service to school, coincidentally the same trophy won by Allan Bradshaw the year before, in its inaugural year. Other than that, I can only say I really enjoyed my time at John Port School even though I did not achieve academically what I should have achieved. Still, *'cest la vie'* as they say in Derby! The next stop would be Birmingham and strangely enough I have stayed in Brum ever since.

College and a Taste of Independence

Having left school, moved away from home, it was 'off the leash' and into College for the next three years and like many eighteen year olds who had not been away for any length of time, the new freedom was to prove potentially explosive. It was also the prelude to growing up, managing on your own the following everyday activities; money, washing, food and most important of all, managing your social life. Oops, and one's education!

But, just before College, and having left school, there was this interlude at Butlins' holiday camp, Skegness. Well, Edinburgh Dining Hall to be precise, and what a lark that proved to be. Perhaps 'lark' is too strong a description, but certainly Jake, my mate from school and I, had more fun, got up to more mischief and into more trouble, than at any time prior to our Butlins' experience. As young waiters we were pitched without any experience or training, straight into the manic meal-times that were to be our life for the next six weeks. Tables cleaned and laid out with crockery, side plates, cups and saucers, salt, pepper and sauces all before the devouring hoards of 'campers' were to descend for their breakfast, lunch or dinner, not once, but for two whole sittings. In peak weeks it felt like three sittings when the camp was full to bursting point. The further away from the serving area, or closer to the punter's door a waiter was the quicker the waiter had to be. That honour, of the fastest and most proficient waiter fell to a Brummie called 'Adge'. He was really Harold and was about fifteen years older than we were and was bloody good at his trade. I was placed next to him for some reason, on table number two for my sins. The setup was that we had eight tables of four people to serve, as quickly and efficiently as possible, all in forty-five minutes to an hour. When that finished we had to shoo them out and get rid of them, lay up again the empty tables and get the next lot of campers in and through, three times a day, seven days a week. And the pay I hear you ask? Six pounds, seven shillings and sixpence a week, before tax! But that was easily doubled with tips added on, and, in a good week we'd be well past double figures. Living like lords, up all hours, mixing with the campers, most of whom when they recognised us off duty, were incredibly generous. Mackesons took a hell of a hammering during those six weeks I can say for sure.

However, life wasn't always straight forward and hunky-dory though in the camp and there was a down side. For example one night a collection of us blokes with girls, were dancing in one of the ballrooms and performing a line dance, blokes in one line, the girls in the other. Mistake number one: don't let the drunken chief redcoat, the camp's hunk and top wrestler, bump into you as you dance. Mistake number two: don't be the tallest on the dance floor and possess a proboscis like mine. It is a target, as they say. Mistake number three: don't carry on dancing when the shit with the biggest shoulders in Christendom, the largest and most muscular arms and most massive fists, wants to talk with you! That was me, but, keeping my hands in my pockets I just about prevented myself from being the first British astronaut into space, without a rocket! Strangely, the following morning on our way to work, we passed the 'Supershit' and he never recognised me. Aah scare baby!

Back in the dining room the most irritating drawback was removing the campers from their tables when they had finished eating, talking and drinking. You were not allowed to set up again whilst they were at their places and even more irritating was when some little bleeder asked his mum for some more soup, after everything had been cleared away and off the table. However, 'Adge' came to my rescue with that one, recommending that I poured the 'extra soup' to the front of the little bleeder's soup bowl so quickly that the soup splashed over the edge of the bowl and onto little Lord Fauntleroy's lap. Ha! Ha! Ha! Served them right and surprise, surprise, they never asked for more soup again at such an undesirable moment.

The positives always outshone the negatives though, in the camp - helped by the ladies from Finland, who had come over to Skegness working at Butlins in droves, almost as if Finland had closed for the summer. Tuula, Uula, Ulla, Kristina, Oona and Venla were some of the Finnish blonde, blue-eyed ladies who passed us the food for the campers from behind the serving hatch and made life much more bearable in the dining room for us youngsters. Talking of ladies, it may be best to mention poor old 'Adge' again here who became embroiled with a lady who is best described as having 'a huge appetite'. Only this appetite was for sex and with 'Adge' particularly. On several nights when 'Adge' was 'in hiding', Jake, me and a couple of other guys tried to find this lady to ask her to back off from our mentor, but we were unsuccessful. We were, of course, aiding 'Adge' because when she caught hold of him the poor sod was knackered for days after. Looking for her was always like looking for a bed-bug in a duvet, something, I bet, that young lady never did, or had time for! Well, not with her past-time anyhow. I often wonder what happened to Adge though. Is he still alive, or, if that lady found him, is he plain worn out? Let me know Adge if you are out there somewhere!

The food Jake and I had was usually the same as the campers, but when we occasionally wandered out for the night and needed to relieve our hunger, we would join the campers who, by now, were eating again in one of the many available cafes. Join the queue, collect a baguette then a drink and wander off to eat at a nearby table was the normal order of events, no matter how long the queue. That is, until we met up with some Scousers who re-educated us in the 'Scouse Way' of queuing, as it existed in 1964 at Butlins'. This was their methodology. Join the queue, decide what you were going to eat, be it a roll, baguette, sausage-roll, pork pie, jam tart etc, and when the queue dwindled and you approached the till, make sure you had eaten your meal and were just ready to pay for the drink you had in your hand. Simple, even when you were just about to go and earn another two and sixpence working on Camp Security!

Me, and my mate Jake, who was at Butlins with me were away from home for the longest time of our lives at that time, working in the camp. Like many friends from school we played winter and summer team games together, had been on County Football training weeks together, he eventually becoming the very successful First Eleven school football captain in our final year. When not playing football we had often socialised at parties, been to local bars in our villages, had worked together on various building sites and had generally enjoyed each others company. It was therefore no problem going to work together, having fun and saving some money for college and university whilst at the Butlins' Skegness establishment. Sadly, when the 'A' level results came out, Jake went to Bangor University and read Mathematics, eventually working in the IT field, and, until we met years later at a school reunion our paths never met again. Why? I went on to P.E. College in Birmingham and stayed there to teach after qualifying, seldom returning to Derby. At our school reunion in 2006 we picked up a brief conversation as if we had been together the day before, and the only thing missing between us .... was the hair on our heads!

From August at Butlins to St Peter's College, Birmingham in September 1964 and a completely different lifestyle. Well, so I thought at first. For me the change was daunting to begin with, particularly the confident senior students and the college lecturers whose style was to walk in, lecture, and walk out, not teach. 'If you can do, if you can't, teach, and if you can't teach, lecture' sprang to mind, and here I was, about to enter into that same abyss of non-productive capitalism. Unless ......

My first day in college was different to say the least. It all began with me meeting a young man who would eventually become my brother-in-law: John William Mitchell, 'Mitch', a day student from Castle Bromwich, Birmingham. Standing inside the Porter's Lodge that first day, watching the world pass him by, his favourite pastime in college, he called me over and greeted me like some long lost friend. Just as I was beginning to wonder who he was he said we had played football against each other on Boxing Day 1963, in Coventry, he for Warwickshire and me for Derbyshire. He reminded me that we lost 4-3 but that I scored all the goals past him, the Warwickshire goalkeeper! Later that same day I met Dick Grogan, who also said he knew me, as we too had played football against each other, him for Lancashire at Oldham. We, Derbyshire, had won 4-3 this time and he said I'd scored a lucky headed goal in the game and as it turned out he was marking me!

Hey Teacher, You're 'aving a Larf

In college, despite his Captaincy of Blackburn Rovers Youth Team, he became known as 'stroller' long before George Graham adopted Dick's mantle! But, how unusual was that to meet two former adversaries on the same day, from different parts of the country? I can remember that game vividly at Boundary Park, because I had played out wide on the right wing that day for some inane reason, and was always falling down in my new boots when, from out of the crowd, came a lone, loud and dreary voice

'Tha's allus on thy arse, number seven!'

Charming beggars in the Oldham crowd that day. Those two students became close mates and we went on to share quality time, and a brilliant holiday in Greece in our Second Year. The holiday was meant to be a very intellectual and educational month away studying, but it wasn't. After all, we were students!

The First Year at college in those early days was mostly forgettable, some would say unforgivable for all the reasons I am not prepared to divulge as members of my family may be reading this! As new students, on our first day we all had to meet in the main college lecture theatre and be greeted by the student union council members. They were just in the process of introducing themselves when a phone started ringing, close by. Eventually the President of the Student Union asked 'Is there a Mr Gordon here, if so could he collect a telephone number from me afterwards, from a young lady?' So embarrassing I did not know where to hide myself. After much laughter from the new students, I eventually discovered the lady to be a 'friend' from Butlins.

Moving on, relationship-wise I was a failure in my First Year with the ladies. Heaven be grateful that I still had P.E. to attend so I could work my socks off and not my pants. When lectures began it was, of course, no coincidence that college social life expanded hugely. There was a large city to explore and two First Division football teams to watch on Tuesday and Wednesday nights. There were College teams to train with, and of course, begging letters to write to the family as the money from my grant flushed out of my bank account like water down a loo. There were dances we had to attend at the other Midland colleges, where we would flat-footedly, and out of time, attempt to woo young ladies. After all, our college was an all-male college! Our own Fresher's Ball seemed to be a great success that first year, 1964. The group on stage that night if I remember correctly were the Chicken Shack who are still on the circuit today. Dances at Birmingham University, where all the top pop groups played, were hugely attractive not only with their own students but for all the affiliated colleges too. A major attraction was the Wednesday night trip into town for 'grab a granny' night at the Locarno which seemed to appeal to some students, but not this one! Whatever did they mean when they grabbed a granny? I have had to wait until my grand daughter, Ruby, was born to join that club.

Friendships with students strengthened as we and practised and then played our matches on Wednesday and Saturday afternoons. Lectures on Saturday mornings often till twelve noon preceded the Saturday afternoon matches. I might add there was much huffing, puffing and swearing on those mornings followed by the fastest emptying of lecture rooms I ever did see as students fled to their coaches taking them to games. As students' confidences increased, Saturday morning lectures became a joke in later years. Poor attendance meant a register of names had to be taken. It was often the case that, instead of a hundred and twenty students being present, as the register should have shown when called, there would only be twenty students in the lecture theatre! Those of us that answered to those one hundred names, on a particular Saturday might perhaps have been better at ventriloquism, rather than teachers, our efforts were so convincing. However, the Principal, on the one Saturday he attended, on raising his eyes to check our numbers, must have been apoplectic, witnessing the very poor attendance, poor bloke.

The routine of college life was so different from life at home. Most students had rooms of their own in a variety of different types of building. Some, built in 1854, were arranged around the Quad containing the 'Holy Acre' desecrated in 1967 by Dave Savage as a token of his love for the college! Newer rooms were built and situated in buildings around the perimeter of the college field as the college numbers grew over the years. Some students were in digs of varying kinds mainly close to the college, a fate that I was to suffer with two mates in our third year.

First Year students were allowed in the main Refectory for breakfast and lunch, but, for dinner had to attend their own dining hall a short distance away. The college meals were legendary amongst the students for their poor quality and for the quantity of leftovers. We didn't lose too much weight though because, less than half a mile away, the College Café did a roaring trade in sausage and bacon sandwiches, as well as making a fortune from the pin-ball machines.

We students collected our mail from the Porter's Lodge, along with horse racing tips, from the College Porter. That was until Bill Harris and me again received a warning from the Vice Principal, advising us that it was not the expected thing for young gentlemen to place bets on horses, and that we would be suspended were we to err again. How times have changed. In this Twenty First Century we would probably have any one of a number of betting companies sponsoring us through college! Yes, how times have changed.

That first term whistled by, and before 'going down' for the Christmas holiday we held the annual Smoking Concert, an end of term variety show staged by the students. Acts ranged from amazingly good to the mediocre, and those badly affected by alcohol. Had I performed in those shows I'd have been pathetic because I could not act for toffee. Well, not in those days. Too much whisky whilst watching that first show, Teacher's whisky of course meant that the end-of-term meeting the next morning with my personal tutor 'Chuck' Berry, was a disaster. I could not remember anything about it! Being at home that Xmas was not the merriest time of my life. My parents were about to separate and divorce and I was working in the same hospital as both them and their friends. That was not easy to say the least, but the auxiliary nursing work provided a necessary diversion and a necessary supplement to my puny college grant. There were school friends to visit and the increasing knowledge that my sisters were growing up and spreading their wings too.

Back at college in the New Year, we began preparations for day-release teaching practice. We had to learn how to write in a 'lesson preparation' book so we all had the same plan to work to. We then had to deliver a one hour 'trial' lesson to 35 to 40 eight year olds, and their teacher, in front of six or seven fellow students and a tutor. Back at college that same evening, after our 'trial' in the classroom, we then had to dissect the worth, or worthlessness, of that particular lesson. This was repeated weekly (or should it be weakly?) until all the students had delivered their lesson and had it dissected. Two points here worth noting: firstly, neither the tutor nor the classroom teacher showed us before, or after, how a lesson SHOULD be taught. Secondly, the students, back at base, hardly said a word in the discussion session about that day's observed lesson in case THEIR performance was trashed at a later stage. Whilst all this was happening the college functioned normally: ladies were allowed to visit their boyfriends on Wednesdays from 4.00pm and Saturdays from 12 noon. On both days, the ladies had to be at the Porter's Lodge, and out of college, by 10.00pm. No wonder they used to put a special powder in our tea to slow us down! Mind you, the Sunday salad tea, with the limp lettuce, perhaps served as a warning when our 'escorted' sat with us in the Refectory!

For my second term at college I managed to acquire a Lambretta scooter, funded by Nana Swindells of course, in the belief that I would go home more often and reduce my expenses. In fairness, it started off that way, and testing the hypothesis, a couple of weeks later I travelled home ....to beg for more money. Weeks later, I had just been ditched by a girlfriend, (too much lettuce no doubt) and so went home for Easter, and more work at the hospital.

Returning to college after the break, I was caught in a heavy rain storm, which caused 'a pickle' near Branston, Burton-on-Trent. Pulling over into a lay-by on the A38 main road, as my scooter's engine began to splutter, I stopped to let the engine cool down, and became totally soaked, in my best waterproofs, whilst waiting for the downpour to finish. Do waterproofs ever function properly? I still ask myself that today. I tried to start the engine again after another wait. Splutter, splutter. So it was off with the side panel and the engineer in me began to explore the possibility of finding, and cleaning, the contaminated, thimble-sized, carburettor. On removing said carburettor, blowing out some sediment and then replacing it, I felt confident in taking out the spark plug to give that a clean too. Little did I know that, when replacing the spark plug, I had got it completely cross-threaded which I found, to my cost, an hour or so later. Nevertheless, when the storm subsided, I tried to start the engine, which this time didn't splutter, so I recommenced my journey back to Brum.

All was well until I was a about mile from college, and I negotiated a long, downhill bend near the Brookhill Pub. It was, by now, a magnificent, sunny Sunday evening, the rain having stopped completely and the road and pavements were drying out. Purring along I noticed four Sikh gentlemen were enjoying a stroll on the pavement as I passed by on the other side. Suddenly, an almighty loud bang, complete with an exploding metal sound, rent the mild Sunday evening air asunder. The Sikhs all hit the pavement, flat out on their bellies, and my scooter spluttered to a halt. Gingerly, I dismounted my scooter, parked it carefully by the side of the kerb and began to scout the area for evidence of what had caused the metallic noise. Immediately, I found the problem. There, in the middle of my scooter's side panel, was a very large hole. I knew immediately what the trouble was. Examining the immediate vicinity I found another culprit on the pavement on the other side of the road in front of the four Sikhs. There was the confounded spark plug that had caused me grief near Burton. I ran over the road, picked up the offending spark plug, apologised to the Asian gentlemen, bid them farewell, ran over to my scooter and started to push it up the hill, back to college. I did not try to replace the spark plug again! The whole incident took only seconds and was over in a flash. Afterwards I was able to laugh my head off about the whole saga: I hope the Sikh gentlemen were too.

Not all my scooter trips were so bad: travelling to Stratford with Roger Elliot and Barrie Corless seemed to take an eternity, at thirty miles per hour, but was worth the effort in the end despite the fact we turned around and went straight back to college. Going into the new, and developing, Brum was another trip that was popular with the scooter boys, who were also known to deviate to more notorious parts of the city! On the whole the scooter experience was worth the hassle. The Lambretta proved its worth, gave pleasure and was easy to operate and cheap to run. It was also, when parked at college, a simple ploy to meet with the Vice-Principal's daughter. Two more scooter *sorties* were to cause me big problems. The back wheel came off and overtook me as I returned from a shift at the Hospital one day. That incident resulted in me just avoiding going underneath the local double-decker bus on its way to Derby. I slid right across the road, picking up a long, nasty graze to my right leg on that occasion. More dangerous was the blow-out in my front tyre, and my head-on collision with a Derby Corporation trolley-bus on my way to a meal at friends. Fortunately I was wearing my PC Plod look-alike helmet which saved me from serious injury. My dinner-date friends helped me push the scooter back to their house, where as far as I know, my scooter resides to this day since they emigrated to South Africa a couple of years later and never returned to the UK to live.

Back at college, in the summer term, all efforts were geared towards our first long, teaching practice in Junior Schools: the real reason we were at the college in the first place. Slow to begin at first, but a brilliant experience all round, it ended all too quickly and that enjoyable teaching interlude, with Junior School children, was over as my focus now would be on teaching secondary pupils. The rest of the college term simply whizzed by and soon we were second year students and almost half way through the course.

Looking back now, playing for the College Second Elevens at football and cricket was a good experience for me as it increased my determination to achieve more the following year. The occasional First Team chances were rare, as many students had played, or were to play, professional football. One had even played in two FA Cup Finals. The cricket team contained first class county players too, and as two were opening fast bowlers, I had to wait for my chance another year. Academically, I did not do any more than I needed to: 'just enough' sums it up really, but I got the grades required to stay on another year and with no warnings.

I did though test one theory in my First Year having been put up to it by a couple of friends on my PE course. It went as follows: 'Is the marking of student essays and work, and therefore the grades that students in Physical Education achieve, influenced by the favouritism of the marker towards the student?' After my first-hand experience in testing the theory out the answer was a resounding 'Yes!' What did I do to test the theory? I took a straight 'A' Grade Child Study, written by a former student and copied it word for word with the exception of the child's name, and of course I signed my own name on the piece of work. I was awarded a 'C' Grade. I had proved the theory. Perhaps I should have smiled more at tutors. That type of favouritism and the allocation of grades would crop up again in my final year when I challenged a tutor about the awarding of specific subject grades in PE that influenced our final marks.

The year finished on a high note, or two, and several of us were richer for having attended the 1965 Erdington Summer Carnival. How come? We were asked to be body guards for a little known Welsh singer, called Tom Jones. Well 'That's Not Unusual' is it? My mate Cedryn, a valley boy himself, was all over the poor 'boyo' like a rash so he was. He must have asked Tom Jones to write his autograph hundreds of times for his Mam, Dad, sister and Aunty Jane, Dai the brush, Gerry the bus etc. etc. Still ten bob is ten bob and was a good student night out. Come to think of it now, the only threat posed to the singer that night was from his body guards! First Year now over the approaching Second Year in college would change my life forever, though I did not know it at the time!

The Second Year was to progress much the same as the First: lectures, lunch, lectures, tea, team practices and the occasional trip to the Country Girl pub, for a pint and the most amazing cheese and onion rolls. At the weekends there were Saturday night dances, college football matches and football matches on Sunday mornings for Fort Rangers F.C. based in Erdington. The latter was run by two butchers and players were from the top amateur leagues, except for one player Eddie Pudie, a local semi-professional. I was lucky to play in that team with two students from college John Cockin, who went with Phil Woosnam to the USA and Atlanta University, and Dick Grogan who had captained Blackburn Rovers Youth prior to college. The games were different from my previous football experiences but the reward, a large steak to take back to college, was well worth it. The best match I ever played in for them was at Edgar Street v Hereford in the Sunday FA Cup. I scored two goals in extra time and we won 8-6. Master-minded by Brian Kenning, a local player, the usual bacchanalian celebrations took place on the way home. That's what I was told at least.

Prior to Xmas 1965, I was taken very ill with ringworm on my tongue. Undercooked pork caused the problem, or so the College matron told me. Off lectures for a couple of weeks, friends would dump their kit in my room, and leave i there, as they attended lectures each morning. Some brought me a small can of soup, the contents of which were easy to swallow, as I was not eating solid food, and of course, they checked on my progress. One bitterly cold morning Billy Harris, a real nutcase if ever there was one, had a later lecture than the others and, to keep warm, as the heating was already off, sat and then lay next to me on my bed. When my door opened it was the Matron on her rounds who came into my room for the usual tongue check, and to see if my worm had disappeared. Seeing the two of us there on the bed, me asleep, Billy peeing himself with laughter, she went apoplectic and left the room screaming and wailing like a banshee. Needless to say the ensuing College enquiry, led by the Vice Principal, concluded that Billy and I had a 'problem' and recommended we should be suspended! The PE lecturers apologised to us immediately, knowing that the whole incident had been blown out of all proportion and was bloody stupid. But that same night, having left the college and standing on New Street station with twenty friends who were seeing me off home was really spooky. But stranger still was the V.P., the force behind the suspensions, on the platform opposite waiting to greet his daughter who was returning from college in the north: the daughter that I had a crush on. Billy? He stayed the night with his girlfriend and future wife, Christine, at her college on the other side of Birmingham, before leaving for their Xmas break.

The following day, the student body met in College and voted to strike if the whole episode was not erased from our records: only one person was to abstain from the vote. Months later, the Principal apologised to me for the whole waste of time, so we were cleared of any untruths that might have, unfairly, ruined our college records. The episode gained me a new room in college, right next to the gymnasium and PE lecture room etc, in the newest residential block, so all was not lost.

The start of the new term and 22nd January 1966 in particular, was to become a very, very important day in my life. It was a Saturday and as usual I had played football, but this time scored six goals in a college game. That night at the college dance, there was the chance of dancing with girls from the nurses' homes or ladies' colleges nearby. The bar was open and, having scored so many goals celebrations were in order. Eventually leaving the bar with a student, Brian 'EB' Jones and walking down the main corridor towards the dance hall, we confronted two beautiful, young ladies. One I had known previously, but not the other young and stunning lady. As I write, we have now been married for thirty eight long years having been together ever since. (I had to write this as she may read this book one day!)

Life would never be the same again and changed and for the better, honestly! I never knew that travelling on the 28 Birmingham Corporation Bus could be so romantic. Or that walking in front of Barrie Corless's little green Morris van, in a pea-souper fog along the

Chester Road in Birmingham all the way to Anstey PE College for women, would also be romantic, as I walked to meet Avril. The trips down to the Red Lion pub were memorable, so I'm told. Ah, romance was not dead in 1966, even if it was all made possible with a ten bob note!

Back at college, work was piling up and another teaching practice was fast approaching, this time in a Catholic secondary school in East Birmingham. But, first and foremost, academic course deadlines had to be met. The midnight oil was being burnt most nights to cram in my PE coursework, Geography coursework, field work, team practices and now, Avril. Trips home were becoming scarcer as the work piled up. Family letters were not always replied to. I was becoming snowed under, but then, so was virtually every other Second Year student. This was the hardest of the three years and would culminate in an Educational Field Trip to Greece.

Firstly, the coursework had to be completed: in PE I was satisfied I had done my best. Secondly, in Geography, the field work, which I really enjoyed, comparing the infrastructure and facilities on two different housing estates, was also finished. I enjoyed conducting my research at the time and it was only when it was assessed and the tutor accused me of plagiarism, marked my work down, and would not change his mind, that I became angry. Despite my appeals and protestations, little changed, and I did not get the high grade I thought I had merited. I did gain my revenge on the lecturer, by spoiling one of his presentations, before we entered the Final Year. I shuffled his lecture notes around when he left the room at a 'toilet break'. He lost his place and I knew he would not be able to carry on without them he was such a bad ad-libber! Damn me, he even wrote 'pause for laughter' in those notes when he cracked one of his feeble jokes! It was naughty of me, I know, but without him that department was excellent and I did deserve much better. Maybe I was just sore at his inability to tell me from which work, book or essay, I had supposedly plagiarised my work.

Team practices continued, and games played, despite the lectures and the teaching practice at Archbishop William's School. I really enjoyed those weeks and when the school play, The Wizard of Oz, was performed, Avril and I were able to attend. It was lucky that one evening, during the practice, I was able to take pupils to a recording studio, in the Bull Ring, that belonged to the father of a friend from college. It just so happened that on that evening, a group called The Move was recording while we visited: the girls in the party went potty over them. Our College Principal went potty, too, one Saturday night at college, when the same group carried on performing after midnight and he couldn't get them off the stage. Tut! Tut!

There was also our Second Year Field Trip, in PE, to endure, where our main objective was to undertake instruction and gain a Basic Mountain Leadership Certificate, at Plas y Gwynant in Snowdonia. All the PE students were away together, and although split into groups, met for meals at night, if not on expedition. The week was good, though very wet, and the fun, companionship and interaction we had in the group was outstanding. Most memorable though, was the expedition I was involved in, when the main aim was to walk over Mount Tryfan, and camp close to Milestone Buttress, which we would climb the following day. The deluge of water in the streams and rivers didn't help, as we set off. Soaked to the skin, in waterproofs, before we had gone ten yards out of the hostel gate, things could only get better. Only they didn't. Crossing one stream as a group, the raging torrent, not only looked formidable, but eventually gave us, undoubtedly, the best laugh of the week. The stream was twenty yards wide by the time we arrived and had to cross it. The crossing point was a place with large boulders, like stepping stones, and where they were missing, we manoeuvred some into place in the stream, to make it easier to cross, so we thought. The farce that ensued was pure Laurel and Hardy comedy. I laughed so much it was difficult to know whether my face was wet with rain or tears of laughter! Several of us, with increasingly heavy backpacks, crossed sensibly, one at a time, over the stepping-stone boulders, just pausing, if a boulder rocked back and forth with our weight on it. Arriving safely on the opposite bank, we took off our backpacks, and waited for the others to cross. Next it was 'Tricky Dicky' Grogan's turn. Gingerly, and with fear in his eyes, he moved towards the first stepping stone and .... just froze. Dashing back across to help, Cedryn and I ushered, cajoled, pushed and pulled him slowly over to the other side. That left one person on the opposite bank, Roger Stanley Elliot, who was possibly the most gifted rugby player of his generation in college, but completely barmy off the field and just about to prove it, where he was standing.

Not feeling confident enough to walk over the stepping stones with his backpack on, he decided to take it off, and proceeded to swing it violently round and round his body, and with a final flourish …… let it go. Nine of us on the other bank stood staring in amazement, as the backpack sailed upwards, but not outwards. We raised our eyes upwards, into the rain, following the arc of the backpack's flight. Of course, it landed in the torrent and hurtled downstream at a rate of knots, too fast for us to catch it and fish it out. For the life of me, I cannot remember if the backpack was retrieved. All I know is that, with typical lunacy, we have never let Roger forget his howler down the years! The rest of the week was to fly by and, though exciting, never matched the quality of the folly that befell our expedition group at that stream crossing. Even so, we all passed and gained the Preliminary Mountain Leadership Certificate – even Roger!

The summer term started, and again seemed to flash by. All this time, Avril and I progressed as a couple and my soon-to-be separated parents were to meet her at a College Open Day for the first time. Later, in the summer holidays, I would meet her parents for the first time, in Gorleston-on-Sea, Norfolk. The relationship was now getting serious!

That summer holiday was interesting: I was able to secure casual work on a building site in Lichfield, Staffordshire, travelling each day with my old junior school mate, Allan Bradshaw. I was able to park my scooter at his girlfriend Linda's house, whilst we travelled by mini bus to the building site. The pay for a student was excellent and most welcome. The

Hey Teacher, You're 'aving a Larf

work not too bad either. That hot summer, working outside with shirts off enabled both of us to acquire deeply tanned torsos, just in time for my trip to Greece. Having finished a couple of month's casual work it was time to visit Greece and study their Education system. Helping me with that research were once again, 'Tricky Dicky' Grogan and John 'Mitch' Mitchell, neither exactly hell- bent on studying Greek Education. Poor me! We had negotiated the study previously with the Education Department in college. They had sanctioned our plan of action and methodology! Little did the authorities, at college, know that the plan would change dramatically from the negotiated original educational suggestions we had planned. Oh dear. In the August of 1966, and after a successful Football World Cup making England World Champions, the three of us left Blighty for Greece. Once there, the temperatures were to take our breath away as they remained throughout our stay in the low hundreds. After a very hot first night's stay in an Athens hotel and then further nights on a hotel roof- top in downtown La Plaka, we vacated the city the city of the Parthenon for cooler climes. Travelling by tramp-steamer around the Cyclades, stopping off at Naxos first, for a few days to swim, we eventually travelled to Mykonos and other islands before we returned to Athens. The last ferry ride into Athens was amongst the animals in cattle class, and I do mean goats, pigs and chickens! Back in Athens and with little money or enthusiasm for the heat in the city, we decided to sell some blood, and use the cash to buy little luxuries, like food! What a 'mistaka to maka'. Lying in a hospital room with road vibrators pounding away just outside the open window, making dust a national entertainment we eventually met with a doctor and several medical students who entered our room, whom we understood were to collect the blood. Discussing their options in Greek, we thought, as they moved amongst us eyeing us up like cattle meat, they chose Dick for their first 'skin puncturing' and blood letting. How many people were in that room at that time I have no idea, what I do know is that three English student teachers were gripped by nervous panic. Who was to go first? Who would they choose? How much blood would they take? Remember Tony Hancock and the 'Blood-donor'? Blind panic, giggling and those immortal words from 'Tricky Dicky'

'What are they doing now, Loz?', as they circled his bed like vultures in the desert waiting to pick over the entrails of a body.

The other two had blood taken from them first, about a pint, and then the Greek medical students were shown my arm. The task they had before them must have been to locate a vein in my arm, or not, as the case turned out. They practiced on my arm several more times as it became punctured beyond recognition, looking like the 'top twenty' on a dart board, and at last having taken my blood, left the three of us to recover. With the 'blood money' in our wallets we strolled back into the centre of Athens ready to eat. We were now rich beyond belief, (should that be relief?), having pocketed £3 each and could afford one of the famous Greek nine-egged omelettes, with chips of course.

On the plane home, it was plainly (sic) evident we had only a little Greek educational information necessary to show for our stay in Greece. We were going to have to put together one hell of an account very soon, with great difficulty. Unless that was the library at college could supply us with the information we should have already acquired, we could supplement it with some post cards of statues around Greece so hopefully we might survive. How we were to eventually pass that test and gain the required grade for our collective work I have no idea. Have they read it I thought at the time or was it one of those pieces of work that would keep an Education Lecturer warm on a cold winter's night? And I meant in his hearth, not heart. We did pass and so the Third and Final year beckoned us.

That final year I lived 'in digs' with two reprobates: William Spencer Harris and Colin Gould, in Alum Rock, Birmingham. I had a small room to myself and the other two had a large double bed. The digs were comfortable and almost warm and the 'lady of the house' looked just like the Deputy Headmistress in 'Please Sir' the old goat. Her 'full' breakfasts of sausage, egg, bacon, black-pudding, fried bread, beans and tomato sound really appetising, if you list the food quickly. The reality was that the whole lot floated and swam around the plates in deep fat. Billy's idea, which Colin and I accepted, was that we place them carefully on the fire whilst the others kept the landlady talking away from the action. Those breakfasts kept the fire alight on cold mornings longer than the coal! After that getting to college was a must as we made haste to get any breakfast leftovers in the Refectory to make up for our loss at the digs. At night, the watery coffee we were given, (she had the proper darker stuff herself), and the single layered, exactly one inch across coconut macaroon we were allowed to have for supper at the digs, leeched into our stomachs and began swishing around like storm-water in an empty drain as we lay in our beds.

With only lectures in Education and Physical Education in our final year life should have been more relaxed. Allocating time for visits to our final Teaching Practice placement, collating information for various essays in Education and putting together final assessment data in PE meant life was still manic. In PE the assessments now counted towards our final grades in the summer of 1967. Trying to improve grades in weak areas was proving difficult for me, particularly my gymnastics and swimming, but I was determined to progress and rapidly if possible. My final teaching practice of eight weeks was based at Sheldon Heath Comprehensive and again I was to share time with 'Mitch'. We were under the guidance of Norman Eve the school's Head of PE and a man who became very helpful to both of us. The school had four gyms each with a huge array of equipment, and with one games field on site and another, a short walk away, they were enough to keep two PE students active for eight weeks, up to Xmas 1966. We were teaching alongside a mature Geography student from college, Jim Chidler, who with his wife Pat introduced me to my first Indian curry meal. Years later Jim and I taught alongside each other at Smith's Wood School, Chelmsley Wood. Jim had entered teaching late having studied Geology at university previously, and had been involved in drilling all over the UK, but with children .... well he changed career to stay nearer home. Time was moving quickly now: the end of the practice arrived and 'Mitch' and I went to thank the Head-teacher for allowing us our teaching practice at his school. The Head's send off left us both confused. He told us we were obviously good students but he thought we were foolish for leaving school just prior to Xmas and missing taking our 'A' Levels. As the penny dropped with us, we explained that we were in fact college students and had been on teaching practice, shook his hand, left his office and went back to college! And that man ran a very large school……...

The last two terms were again very busy and included a field trip to Hadrian's Wall for Mitch and me as our final piece of PE assessment. Walking the Wall was challenging, so a stop overnight to recuperate next to the inn at Twice Brewed was most welcome. Carlisle slipper baths were even more welcoming and acceptable even if there were some 'funny' people cleaning themselves the afternoon we arrived. The only blot on the whole trip had been a lift we accepted in a lorry going north. It just had to be driven by a Scottish driver, and Scotland football supporter, on the day Scotland beat the World Cup holders at Wembley. The result was that Scotland beat England 3-2 at Wembley. Pah!

Acquiring an FA coaching award in football, an MCC coaching award in cricket, coaching awards in athletics and basketball were compulsory now that litigation was beginning to have a major impact in school sports, so teaching PE required the top qualifications. Examinations were taken and completed which left the last week in college a bit flat, but with time for reflection over our three year course. The question of tutor assessment cropped up again and particularly how they had arrived at the 'fictitious' marks they awarded each student. I am being cynical again. Not being happy with the perceived injustices amongst some of the grades allocated one of our group of disgruntled students, who must of course be nameless, accessed the whole list of tutor grades from the PE offices in college, the night before our 'leaving dinner'. Yours truly presented this copy before one of the PE tutors on our last night. Naughty, of course it was, but it proved a worthy example of poor educational practice and a good future lesson for young teachers in that they should not have favourites.

A month previously, in May, I had been walking along a main college corridor when the Head of Education appeared next to me, asked me my name and if I had a job to go to. I told him I hadn't applied for a teaching post at that time but would eventually, but wished to stay in Birmingham. He took me to his office, got out his Times Educational Supplement, found an advert in a Warwickshire School at Castle Bromwich and promptly told me his friend, from his own time in university, was the Head-teacher. He made a phone call to the school's Head, I was interviewed, got the post as a PE assistant at Park Hall and have never looked back. My thanks retrospectively go to that most generous of men, 'Happy' Hamnet, the Head of Education at St Peter's college, for his indiscreet act of nepotism.

The prospect of a job was exciting and I looked forward to beginning my teaching career in September, in Castle Bromwich, a commuter suburb outside

Birmingham. Before then, I needed to generate funds to survive my first month in teaching, and find somewhere to live outside of college. That would mean working again during the summer holiday and thanks to Barrie Corless and his family, did just that in Norfolk. With Barrie, and Dave Hewitt, I spent the first week picking strawberries and managing to acquire a skin-allergy brought on by stuffing my face full of strawberries. With millions of spots all over my body I became a pariah amongst friends, but help was at hand. We obtained really well-paid jobs working on the North Sea Gas pipeline construction project, near Kings Lynn, as labourers. Our wages per week after paying tax were almost the same as our first month's wages in teaching. That job with all its money not only enabled me and Avril to become engaged but for me to have some cash to rent a house on returning to Birmingham. And Mrs Corless introduced me to what has become a favourite meal of mine, cauliflower cheese. Mmmmm!

Learning to Teach: Part One

Returning from Norfolk at the end of August 1967, the situation demanded I immediately find somewhere to live, and I realised that it would be cheaper to share. Barrie Corless, Dave Hewitt and I set about hunting for a house. We met a lady teacher called Mo who was also looking for a place to live, and so the four of us moved into a house in Ward End, Birmingham and settled down. Some legal problem or other meant that we had to move to the flat next door. Mo moved out, Cedryn moved in and, by Xmas, we decided to terminate the letting contract and we all went our separate ways. I returned to Castle Bromwich and stayed in a bungalow next to a night club for two weeks. It was owned by the parent of one of my pupils, and although a very comfortable place to live, it was too expensive. Later, I met up again with Dave Hewitt and Cedryn Lloyd and we moved to a large bed-sit in Sutton Coldfield, our home for the next eighteen months, and what a home it was to become!

Park Hall School for Boys, a secondary modern school in North Warwickshire, had been open since the 1950s and the first Head-teacher, George Waite, a big powerful man who had served in the forces during the war, was still in charge. A canny man, he saw fit to give me the Fourth Year leavers as my first tutor group, to cut my teeth on, as I was one of three rookies on the staff. I'm sure it helped, though, that I taught PE and was six feet three inches tall!

My tutor group were the usual misfits: they knew it, I knew it, I knew they knew I knew it, and I knew they were prepared to push the school, and its rules, as far as possible, with me, still wet behind the ears, in charge of them. Put it another way: as I learnt the ropes, they were one step ahead of me, and they knew all the tricks to avoid registration. They brought me convincing notes from home to explain absence or incomplete homework, most probably written by their mates. Even though they were bottom of the pile, going nowhere, they knew more about life than I did at that time. They taught me a great deal including: (1) Don't get too friendly (2) Be tough, but be fair to pupils and (3) Leave the 'emotional' door open, in case they need to enter, to seek help. In other words, keep your distance, but be prepared to meet them halfway to help them, if they need it.

I had one large weapon in my educational armoury to assist my acceptance by them: P.E. was a favourite subject in this boys' school, and I was skilful enough on the games field, and in the gym, to impress them. But then, I should have been able to influence them, just fresh out of P.E. College. Gradually, as the year wore on, some pupils left, permanently, at Xmas; some left at Easter and the rest left in the summer, all at the age of fifteen. We parted on fairly good terms, and for years after they had left, if I saw them in the shops, or bars, in North Warwickshire, we always exchanged cordial greetings, and occasionally the liquid variety as well!

My Head of Department was Terry Smyth, 'Pancho' as I came to call him on account of his Mexican moustache, a rugby playing scrum half, who was of the 'old school'. Nothing wrong with that of course and he taught me a great deal during my four formative years there, encouraging me to develop school sport, in all spheres. The school had an excellent record in sport and had produced many good footballers, athletes and cricketers in years past, and did so for years to come. District and county footballers, district and county athletes and club cricketers at the school, in all age groups, benefited the reputation of Park Hall. With 'Pancho' support, I helped expand the number of football teams, cricket teams and brought basketball on to school representative level. We increased the standard and the amount of training in gymnastics to produce display and competitive teams against other schools and in championships. By the time I left 'Pancho' and I had created two football teams in each year, a cricket team in each year, two basketball teams, two school gymnastic teams and three school athletic teams. 'Pancho' was totally supportive of the expansion programme, and there were sufficient young, and enthusiastic, staff to manage and coach teams. The school House system had very willing, devoted staff as House masters, and they provided sufficient competent schoolboy performers to supply the school teams, as the number on roll increased. The P.E. Department needed more full time staff to cope with the increased numbers and so in 1969 Geoff Rutherforth joined us - a very talented, supremely fit and competent all-round athlete. Successes increased at District and County level and the 1968/9 Fourth Year football team won the prestigious Aston Villa Cup at Villa Park with 'Pancho' as their Alf Ramsay type of manager, for what truly must have been the highlight of their school football career.

'Pancho' had many strings to his P.E. bow, and a passion for skiing in particular. Consequently, every two years, he took parties to Austria, independent of the local authority. My first trip with him and Mike Fox, another staff member, and thirty three pupils, was to a little village called Imst in the Austrian Tyrol at New Year, 1968. To say the trip was eventful is a massive understatement.

Leaving Birmingham by coach to travel to Victoria Rail station early in the morning was never a good idea for young boys or staff, even if they were going skiing, because both become so manic and excited. From Victoria we took the boat train to Dover and then boarded a ferry that took us to Ostend in Belgium, across a very choppy English Channel. On arrival at Ostend the first sign of chaos arose when all pupils suddenly wanted the loos. Unfortunately, they also needed Belgium coins to pass through the turnstiles, to access the toilets. I was particularly impressed when one young man returned with some Belgian coins when he had been to the loo! I was less impressed later when, on the coach travelling through Germany, he informed me that he had placed his hand in the money tray by the entrance to the toilet and wriggled it about, as if putting in a coin, when in fact, he only took coins out! A young man to keep an eye on from then on, I thought. A career as an accountant beckoned, I figured.

The autobahn journey slowed as we hit tremendous snowstorms and blizzards south of Frankfurt, and, after a long journey, we arrived a little late in Imst, the village in Austria to be our home for the next week, including New Year's Day. Interestingly, during the night's journey, we noticed the drivers had changed seats without stopping. Seeing them perform the changeover later, in a blizzard, through half-shut eyes was very nerve-racking. The week in Imst was sensational for skiing and tobogganing as there was so much snow on the ski slopes. The instructors were good too and allowed the pupils to toboggan, as well as ski, after the morning skiing lessons. The ability of the pupils was really incredible and they took to skiing like ducks to water. The days always began with a lesson from the Austrian ski school instructors in groups of six or seven. Practice was extensive, competitive and exhilarating and down a really testing beginners' slope of four kilometres. Lunch of a ham or cheese roll and a very hard boiled egg, accompanied by a 'gluhwein' or two for the staff - kids always had a soft drink - a daily ritual taken in the Untermarkter Alm café near the top of the slopes. The afternoons were semi-free to practice and progress from the morning's instruction, or to try tobogganing. The top and bottom of the slopes were joined by a chair-lift that would often stop suddenly to let people, or blankets, off at the top. This often left skiers suspended in their chairs a couple of hundred feet up over Pancho's aptly named 'Fractured Ass Pass,' an accident zone if ever there was one. It was a difficult point on the slopes where a particularly nasty down hill bend began and many experienced skiers often came a cropper. To this day I don't know why one pupil, above the pass, when we were waiting for the chair-lift to begin moving upwards again to the top of the slope, asked in a very loud and almost musical voice that echoed through the mountains like Julie Andrews,

'Sir, please sir, why has the lift stopped?'
Some questions are just too difficult to answer!

Towards the end of the week the pupils prepared for their ski tests and I know the majority not only performed well, but also impressed the Austrian examiners with their fearlessness on the slopes. That night was New Year's Eve, and when the evening meal had finished and the pupils and staff had finished tobogganing, we bade each other 'Goodnight and A Happy New Year' dispensed the last few Strepsil throat tablets to the needy, and turned off the corridor lights about ten thirty pm as usual. Keeping an eye on them, as we rotated the duty of checking the rooms the pupils appeared to have settled down quietly and quickly and soon Pancho, Mike and I went into the bar for a celebratory drink, or two. A small disco had started in an adjacent room and we were invited to dance as the New Year came in. However, our dancing and celebrations were soon halted by the sight of a pupil at the bar door, who, in his pyjamas, called over to me in a loud 'whisper'.

Seemingly, he and his mates had seen a ghost in their bedroom. Well, that went down like a lead balloon, particularly as I was dancing with the wife of a French MEP, and 'Pancho' and 'Foxy' were dancing together. But not wanting to appear disbelieving of the poor boy, Miles, I followed him upstairs. We passed bedrooms with pupils looking out of doors to see what the commotion on the landing was all about that made our way upstairs to the ghostly room seem even longer, as I ushered them back inside their rooms. One room that I called in along the way had a pupil in it so full of fear, panic and horror that his face was literally ashen with shock. Miles' bedroom was even more in panic: the pupils inside were terrified, having seen something that they had all, apparently, witnessed. After I had calmed them down, one of them explained the following to me: they had been talking as midnight approached when, as the church bells struck twelve, a face appeared at the window and this person was dressed in what was thought to be an old German Army trench coat from long ago. With a long beard and a 'Wee Willie Winkie' hat on his head (their words not mine), an old, tired looking man entered their room via the window, walked across to their wardrobe, opened the wardrobe door and entered it. When one of the pupils opened the door, a mouse ran out, crossed the bedroom floor and left the room via a concrete lintel under the window. Opening the wardrobe door further, when they had stopped shivering with fright, they found that the man had disappeared.

The appearance of that ghost on New Year's Eve was hard to believe, but the boys were all so convincing. I called and collected from downstairs the other two members of staff and on the way back up to the bedroom where the ghost was sighted, filled them in with the story as told to me by the lads in the 'ghost' room. It's not difficult to gauge their reaction is it? The boys in that room and by now other rooms too, were absolutely adamant about what they had seen. Eventually, we managed to persuade the lads to get off to sleep, and we headed back to our own rooms, playfully looking round corners to see if any more spooks were in evidence!

Next morning was chaotic as the story was embellished by the pupils and, try as we might we failed to dampen down their emotional state. One of the pupils, Big Ada, still had a sore throat and we had run out of Strepsil throat tablets in the first aid box. During the course of the week several pupils had had sore throats, and so the supply had depleted more quickly than we expected. This necessitated a trip to the local chemist to replenish stocks. Big Ada said he would go alone and had only been gone a short while when a loud scream pierced the calm atmosphere of Imst village. There, chugging up the hill at a good rate of knots towards the hotel, came Ada, by now aided and abetted by some of his mates who had met him halfway. What the hell was going on?

'It's him sirs,' he shouted hoarsely, 'it's him, honest' as he breathlessly spoke to us three teachers. 'It's the bloke who was the ghost.'

I took Ada back to the chemist's shop to find out who he was referring to. He reluctantly entered with me dragging him in, and pointed to a painting on the wall behind the chemist.

'There he is sir, that's him!'
'That's who?' I enquired.
'The ghost' said Ada, 'the one in our room last night.'

With that, I asked the chemist who the person in the painting was. In perfect English, he told me that a legend in the village decreed that every New Year, the old Doctor came back to the village, on the stroke of twelve o'clock. He had been skiing alone on the slopes, had a dreadful, near- fatal accident and almost bled to death where he fell. Days later he was found by a search party, brought down to the village, and died of his injuries and blood loss. The chemist continued to say that his ghost apparently returned every year to the hotel that he died in, just as the church clock struck midnight. In addition, rumour had it, he returned to the room he died in.

'Which room?' I asked, tentatively.

Stepping out of his shop and pointing to our hotel, he indicated a room on the top floor, right-hand side - the very room that Miles, Ada and the others were in! The hair on my body was now vertical I'm sure, and with an 'I told you so' look, directed at me from Ada, I thanked the chemist and returned to the hotel. Ada was now a hero, the centre of attention, and his mates fired questions at him like a machine gun burst! Pancho, Mike and I went into a quiet huddle, discussed again the facts from the previous night, called the pupils to order, and set off up the slopes for our last ski lessons. In the Untermarkter Alm ski café at lunchtime, we put questions to the ski instructor who taught our boys, about the legend of the Doctor, whose 'gheist' had appeared, so they said, to some of our lads the night before. He completely agreed that it was a true story and, though not verifying the boys' story in full, acknowledged that the locals would all corroborate this annual event.

I can say, in all honesty, that I would trust those lads with my life and down the years, having remained in touch with a couple of them, I have no doubt nor any reason to change my mind.

Two years later, on a similar skiing trip, again to the same hotel in Imst, Pancho and I enjoyed insisting that we could see 'eyes staring outwards' from behind the wooden festival masks that lined the staircase walls. And we also felt the presence of the 'gheist,' who seemed close by, as we walked up the stairway with two new members of staff, Stewart Cooper and Ken Howell, who all but pooed themselves at the mere mention of the word GHOOOOOOOOST!!

That trip was notable for several reasons, but primarily the absence of the snowfalls we had experienced two years earlier, so we had to ski much higher up the mountain than before. The pupils enjoyed themselves, which was the main aim, and gained their ski badges after examinations, many collecting a gold standard.

Whilst at Park Hall several other incidents, I recall, made the job of teaching so enjoyable. I'm not referring to the loss of free periods, taken from us when teaching staff were away ill, or the reaction to that imposition by my Head of Department, as his language was far too 'incendiary' for this book! But I refer to the possible 'skills' of our much loved Head teacher, Mr Waite, who often told Pancho and me and anyone else listening, how he had once canoed 'up' rapids as high as the school gymnasium. A colossal feat indeed for anyone except the SAS, but guaranteed to send Pancho, complete with his Zapata moustache, into fits of giggles and an hourly re-enactment of the Head's story, complete with rowing motions, as if in a canoe, for the rest of that day. 'Have I told you Loz about that time I ….?' I can hear him now.

Other memories of the Head teacher that bring tears to my eyes as I recall them may mean nothing to others, but those who were there will never forget them. Appealing to an Assembly one morning, he told the whole school that the charity collection for the coming term would be in aid of……………

'Blind dogs for the Guides'

This cock-up seemed to pass the schoolboys by, but not the staff, who reacted with the usual bouts of loud sniggering whilst in full view of the school as they sat on the stage behind the Head. But that was nothing compared with the outburst, prior to an October half-term holiday that involved the Head again. The school had become littered with broken conkers after all it was that time of the year. He, the Head, had had enough of all the mess and was now about to tell the assembled throng. Slowly, taking off his glasses and leaning on the lectern, we staff knew something really serious was about to be announced to the pupils. Nothing could have prepared us for what was about to be said next, and the staff who were present that day will never forget the subsequent few minutes.

"Conkers!" bellowed the Head. Immediately behind him several staff fell into the wings of the stage, in absolute hysterics. One Welsh member of staff, who must be nameless, but who now lives near Peterborough, let out such a screech of surprise the Head turned to see what was going on behind him. All he saw were staff hiding their faces, biting their fingers to keep quiet, wiping the tears of laughter from their eyes; and several walking back onto the stage from the wings as if in a Shakespearean 'walk-on' part. The elder schoolboys slowly cottoned on to what had been said and hid their eyes. But what did it mean? In simple terms, in 1969, the Head may as well have stood on the stage for assembly and told all the pupils to 'Bollocks,' such was the interpretation of the word 'Conkers' at the time.

On the day, in 1971, when the Boys school officially closed, prior to amalgamation with the Girls school next door to form a comprehensive school, it just so happened to be the Head's birthday. The Head of Music, in keeping with the demob happy mood at that moment, managed to incorporate into the proceedings the school hymn played with his right hand on the piano and 'Happy Birthday' played with his left hand, at the same time! Clever bloke was our Peter. Magic, fantastic, incredible, amazing, super ……. as Jim Bowen would say!

An unintentional chuckle, at the expense of the Head, occurred following an interview for a job I did not want. In 1971 the Chelmsley Wood Estate was expanding at a rate of knots on the north- east side of Birmingham. New schools were needed to cope with the influx of youngsters, and the Head of the Girl's High School next door, Miss Evans, had been newly appointed as Head of a new school, Smith's Wood, a mile down the road from Park Hall. Mr Waite said I should apply for the Head of Boys' PE at the new school. I was not in the least bit interested and told him I was more than happy to stay put teaching where I was. Talking me into applying for the post, I reluctantly attended an interview with Miss Evans and the Chairman of Governors, Mr Jones. Mr Jones had taught very briefly at Park Hall Boys' School, seemingly almost a full day, and was now an F.E. lecturer. My interview lasted half an hour and consisted of just two questions. The first question asked me to certify who I was and the second question 'Had I any questions?' Thirty seconds had passed, and my question relating to the impending takeover of this part of Warwickshire – would it be Birmingham or Solihull? - took twenty nine minutes and thirty seconds to answer it. End of interview, go to dinner. Whilst I was in dinner with Pancho it was not long before the Head ventured over to ask me how the interview had gone. I told him, truthfully, that I felt it could have gone much better.

Pancho giggled behind his knife and fork. The Head left the room and I thought that was that.

Later that day, after school, I was refereeing a football match and Pancho was running the line for me. Who should come out to the game? That's right, Mr Waite, who then proceeded to follow me all over the football pitch, whilst the match was in progress, telling me that all was fine and that I had got the job at the new school. Pancho nearly collapsed in a heap of laughter as I tried to accelerate away from the Head, but, fortunately, once the Head had succeeded in imparting the successful interview titbit, he went on his merry way.

My final memory of Mr Waite was of his generosity, to myself in particular, but to others as well, as he puffed away on his Capstan Full strength cigarettes. When Avril and I married he was not able to attend the wedding, but he gave us a clock as a present. I couldn't ever remember being late for school, but the clock was fine.

Another character in the school will certainly remain nameless, gave us so many laughs and created so much pandemonium with his behaviour that he became a legend to all who knew him. He was in my estimation, without doubt, one of the most gifted all-round sportsmen that I have ever had the pleasure of trying to avoid! I really did say 'trying to avoid', and at all costs too. An excellent gymnast, superb rugby player, very talented football player, a terrific athlete and a really good cricketer – but, only he could provide the wealth of stories and anecdotes which still bring tears of laughter to my eyes. The stories that abound about him are all true and need no elaboration on my part. I do not have room to include all the tales that I would like to, and the following is but a mere sample, that will live for ever in the memories of those of us that knew him.

New to the department, our friend asked Avril and me to accompany him and his lady friend out for a meal 'on the town' so to speak. Balsall Common near Solihull fitted the bill and T-bone steaks all round were the order of the day. For an aperitif, before the meal, we assembled in a small bar adjoining the restaurant area. Whilst I ordered and took the drinks to the table the ladies and our friend seated themselves on stools close by. Next thing I knew, our friend, with a drink in his hand, performed a perfect backward roll off his stool and landed in the centre of the bar area. He stood up, with stool in hand, as if having performed a gymnastic routine in the Olympics, and cursed us three for not warning him that the stool did not have a back to it! He never spilt his drink then, nor did he on other occasions he performed, and I never knew how! I sometimes spilt my drinks either through having had too much or tripping over an obstacle in the bar. Not him, he was a pure genius at falling over and standing up with a full glass of beer, however he fell over!

On another occasion after night-school, whilst having a drink in a local bar, our friend was challenged to perform one of his 'gymnastic and beer' stunts there and then in the middle of the pub lounge as all and sundry looked on. Moving all the tables and chairs back towards the edge of the lounge, he performed a back somersault there and then, in the lounge bar. If that was good, when I tell you that he performed it with a beer glass, two-thirds full, in his hand and never

Hey Teacher, You're 'aving a Larf

spilt a drop, then you must realise how entertaining he was, and what a brilliant gymnast he was too.

With some money in his pocket our friend decided he would like to buy a car, and, by pure chance, the Head of Art had one available: a big automatic Wolseley. Not happy with the automatic gear box, he spent as much money converting the car to a manual gear box as he had paid for the car itself. One problem - the car now had a hole in the floor! On his first trip home to show his mum the new car, accompanied by big Graham, a colleague from school, he went to fill up with fuel and whilst at the garage decided to take his treasured possession through the car wash. He didn't want to show his mum and the people of Yorkshire a dirty car now did he? What a nightmare was about to unfold. Driving into the car wash and seeing the wash rollers moving towards him he panicked and wanted to get out of the car there and then. But decided instead to drop to the feet of his passenger, Graham, and hide in the footwell under the glove compartment, having first dived over the gear stick almost enduring a plastic enema in the process. His undoubted gymnastic ability clearly saved his bacon which he had probably eaten that same morning! Car-wash over, he returned to the driving seat, and headed for Yorkshire, and arrived without further ado.

On the rugby field at Moseley RFC, playing for the 'Knights' on his debut as scrum-half one Wednesday evening, he burst from the base of the scrum and sprinted to score a really good solo try right under the posts. Those of us watching in the stand will never forget the next few moments as he realised he had just scored his first try for a very prestigious club. He performed flick-flacks all the way back to the half way line, took his position ready for the restart of the game, whether or not the conversion was made, and stood and waited. The twenty nine players and the three officials on the pitch who witnessed our friend's performance just gawped in amazement. Now, things like that don't happen very often in rugby, and in all my time as a spectator of that sport, I have never witnessed anything like it before or since. A pity that no TV recording exists of his gymnastic demonstration!

His introduction to the cricket nets at Coleshill CC caused quite a stir too. Keith Bedford, back to play for the club, having been the youngest player to open the batting for Warwickshire CCC was batting in the net our friend was about to bowl in. Our friend bowled six balls at Bedford and clean bowled him on three occasions in one over. Good bowling you ask? Well …. It might have been if the batsman had offered a stroke, or at least, tried to hit the ball, as that is supposed to be the idea. But he was rooted to the spot, transfixed, as all six balls were bowled by a coughing, spluttering, animated bowler who was euphoric, knowing he had clean-bowled a Warwickshire batsman. Sadly he never performed as well for the Second or Third teams.

Prior to entering PE College our friend competed in the All England School Sports as a very accomplished sprinter for his county, Yorkshire. In the 100m he ran and qualified for the second round of heats. This was interrupted by the relay heats in which he ran the anchor leg. Normally at end of a relay race sprinters would hand the baton back to the race officials, and this is what he should have done. As luck would have it though, he had managed to wiggle a finger into the end of the baton and got it stuck there! No amount of wrestling would help free the baton and when the next heat for the 100 metres was called he had no choice but to run the race with the relay baton stuck on the end of his finger! To this day I have no idea how he removed the baton, or how many other races he ran with the same baton on his finger, because, as I was laughing so much, I never heard the end of the story. Or even, God forbid, if he ran with TWO batons in the next relay heat. You could not make it up.

But his capers are not yet ended. He often arrived, unannounced, on Sundays, at the house of some of his colleagues just as they were serving up lunch. This became an annoying ritual that they never really confronted him about, until one Sunday, when the main meal was a curry. He arrived, saw what was on offer, said he loved curry when he knew what was on the menu and proceeded to stuff his face rapidly when his portion arrived on the place mat. But this was no ordinary curry: this curry was made especially for him and for a reason. It was hot, very, very hot, so bloody hot it nearly melted our friend's fork when he inserted it into some smouldering chicken. There he sat choking and spluttering and eventually informed his chums at the dinner table, rather hoarsely, that they could have killed him with the potency of the curry. Well, words to that effect anyway, but guess what? No more did he arrive for his unscheduled lunch at that house. Sad, but that's the way his weekly rendezvous for dinner at that house was terminated.

Lawrence Gordon

But, I hear you say, 'Not more?' Yes, just one more tale and the best of the bunch. I'd left to teach elsewhere, and for a short while, our friend continued at Park Hall Boys' School until he went to teach at a school in Oxford. This had me crying for ages when I was told of it by a good mate who had shared a house with our eccentric and mutual friend. (Graham you really must censor your mouth!) Living in a flat in Oxford, our friend decided to become a participant in that great Seventies British sport of 'streaking'. (running around naked, i.e. without clothes on guys.) Wanting and needing to be part of the craze, he ventured out of the front door of his flat one evening like a young rabbit outside its burrow for the very first time. He looked left and right, to see if the coast was clear, before he set off 'streaking' and then left the flat, closed the door, and bolted down the road to his left, sprinting as fast as his little legs would carry him. At the end of the avenue and halfway round his route, he checked for an audience, turned left again, and carried on sprinting. So far so good, and he was making good progress. Another left turn and, with his flat coming into view, he was nearly home and dry. Arriving at his door, out of breath and sweating with the fear of being caught naked, he suddenly realised that he had dropped a 'bullock'. He had left his key inside the flat and was locked out. What was he to do? End of story!

You may ask why I have included these last few incidents and facts about a colleague who cannot answer back. Answer? Laughter, simply laughter, that's all it ever was. Since we always laughed with him, not at him, he himself laughed with us all the time and never took offence. I have never known any individual make such an impact on people as our friend did in the few short years I knew him. I'm sure I speak for others too when I say that, mention any of the escapades he was involved in, and whether they knew him or not, they would just utter one word. But not here eh, after all, enough is enough.

A feature that was appreciated by the PE staff at the school was the good condition of the school playing fields. The playing fields were extensive and I cannot recall any fixture ever being called off in my time there because the pitches were so well drained. We went out in all weathers for games lessons - snow, wind and rain, every conceivable weather condition. One sad story that happened in the wet occurred one cold morning, after having kitted a pupil out with spare shorts and top. Following the usual drills and practices for football, towards the end of the lesson, we played mini games across the pitches. This one pupil, from a dysfunctional background, was tackled in the course of a game and was accidentally caught on his shin, as his plimsolls skidded into the other pupil's boot on the wet surface.

"You ---- " he cried, and hearing him from thirty yards away, I dashed over, admonished him, sent him off, and told him to wait for me by the P.E. office. Games lesson over, I met him and asked why on earth he used the language he had. He profusely apologised and said to me, in all innocence,

"I'm so f ------- sorry, sir". I tried hard not to laugh but told him he'd let himself down, his parents down and me down by using that language, which I never wanted to hear again. I was delighted when he eventually became District Shot Putt champion and a County Representative, but sadly, he never progressed any further. He failed to turn up for his big athletic day such was the lack of backing from home. Although not too bright, he was a talented pupil ….. If only he'd had a little more help from home.

The last three recollections concern two cricket matches and one Duke of Edinburgh Award story. The first was a cricket House Match after school. I have already mentioned the school had a really sound House System that fed the school teams, and that so many pupils were involved in sport it was good to be part of that system, whether staff or pupil. On this occasion the Head of Science was umpiring, with me at the other end. Up comes the bowler, bowls, the ball strikes the pad and a thunderous shout of 'Owzat' pierced the early evening air. The umpire's (Head of Science) finger shot skywards immediately the call was made, and the batsman was given out LBW. Who I wondered shouted so loudly and appealed? Yes, none other than the aforementioned Head of Science, who by now was turning bright red in the face, like the setting sun.

"Thank you Mr Mahy," I said, "will that be all?"

The second incident at cricket concerned the annual Boys v Staff end of season game. Yours truly, having played in the Birmingham League all summer, went into bat down the order. I needn't have bothered. The first ball I received almost hit the toes of the bowler, ran along the floor of the pitch (a grubber), and hit me in front of my stumps on my big toe. After a whispered appeal from the bowler I was soon marching back to the pavilion having been given out by none other than Mr Waite the Head teacher. Alleluia!

Finally, towards the end of my time at Park Hall Boys, I had been working with a small group of pupils on the Duke of Edinburgh's Award Scheme. Part of the Award was an expedition and so I arranged for it to take place in Wales, close to a village called Corris. The weather was good and we left school on time with Stew Cooper driving the old ambulance, or rather, School bus. We stayed at a cottage run by the St John's Ambulance Brigade and after an evening meal and when the pupils were safe, well fed and quietly ensconced in rooms prior to their big day on Saturday/Sunday, some of the staff, fancying a quick bevy just down the road, visited the local hostelry. Leaving the 'troop' in capable staff hands we drinkers ventured into the village but could not compete with the local vicar who was obviously a member of the Welsh International Drinking Team that year! Not so pissed though when we gave him a lift home, he begged for me to read the lesson in his chapel the next day at Matins, suggesting I re-routed the boy's Duke of Edinburgh expedition so they could hear me read. All went according to plan: I read the Bible lesson in church, witnessed by the boys who then went on to finish a good expedition. The vicar was so happy he arranged to meet us in the village hotel for lunch, knowing he could get a drink there in that 'dry' part of Wales.

Park Hall Boys' School was a very happy period of my life. I thoroughly enjoyed my job, loved teaching the boys, enjoyed the company of the staff and, when I left, I did so with a very heavy heart. I have many friends from that time in my life, both pupils and staff. However, Avril and I were now married and the future looked bright, the future was Smith's Wood School, the future was to be our own family.

Learning to Teach: Part Two

September 2nd 1971 saw the opening of Smith's Wood Comprehensive School, Chelmsley Wood, for pupils in Years One and Two. The First Years came from the local primary feeder schools, and the Second Year pupils came from the surrounding secondary schools but were living in the new school's catchment area. As with all new pupils the uniform was absolutely immaculate and remained so, even after they had been in the Small Hall on that first morning sitting on the floor, waiting to be allocated their new tutor group. The staff appointed to this new school had arrived courtesy of local secondary schools. Only a couple of staff had been appointed from schools outside the county, and in one case, from outside the country. Even so, there was an expectant buzz around the staff and pupils as they began this new educational venture.

For Val Pickard (Long) and me our only problem was the lack of P.E. facilities on site. Thankfully, Park Hall School, my former school, loaned us their outdoor facilities for that first year whilst ours were being completed. Pupils travelled by coach to lessons at Park Hall, and to Woodcock Street Swimming Baths near the city centre. That first year was an eye-opener for me, and the pupils proved so resilient, coping with all the travelling but went on and achieved many awards as a result of our combined endeavours. The swimming awards that were gained more than made up for the hours of travelling by coach to the baths. The First Year boy's football team won the Erdington and Saltley schools Division Two by a mile, and were losing finalists in the District Cup. Cross-country running, round the new school perimeter, became a great trainer for the other sports in this year and provided a number of District runners too.

All things considered, I was pleased with the way the pupils had performed in our first year and looked forward to further developments the following year, when our indoor facilities would be available, including a swimming pool. Avril had given birth to our son Andrew in March 1972; coincidentally the same day as the First Year District Cup Final, and everything seemed to be coming up daisies. Sadly, having collapsed on the games field at Park Hall whilst teaching athletics at the beginning of July, I was nearly pushing up daisies having contracted encephalitis. This shadow over our lives came at the worst possible time for Avril as she realised Andrew had severe developmental problems and I was struggling for my life, but also her mother was recovering, two hundred miles away, from a serious operation.

Back at school in the October, the pupil's prayers for me obviously having worked, the main priorities included ordering equipment for the gymnasium, sports hall and swimming pool, along with the day-to-day equipment necessary to run a PE department. A generous one-off allocation of money enabled Val and I to, not only equip for the coming year 1973/74, but also to allocate and purchase equipment for future years. Whether we made the right decisions or not I'll never know, but we were never short of equipment for the majority of pupils, for years to come. The school began expanding rapidly on this overspill housing estate to the east of Birmingham, and that meant that the Boys and Girls P.E. departments required extra staff. John Price was appointed in 1973 and he brought his national expertise in trampolining and gymnastics to Smiths Wood. He was followed by Andy Stewart in 1974 who added national expertise in outdoor pursuits and athletics. Both these guys contributed massively in all areas of P.E. but their specialities were to have brilliant results with the pupils. In 1979 Ken Taylor joined the department as a really adept coach and motivator of the major games and covered my back as I was teaching P.E. less and less. All were very competent games players and teachers of the major games themselves which only enhanced the potential of the P.E. Department. I felt that the balance of different expertises within the department enabled pupils to have the widest possible

P.E. education. Similarly the Girl's department which had now appointed Miss Hastings (Kendrick), later to become Head of Girl's P.E., and the Misses Fawcett (Cherrington), Gardner and Clarke introduced the pupils to a wide range of activities that also enabled the girls to experience a broad spectrum in P.E.

After school-practices and matches formed a jigsaw of huge proportions, but with cooperation alongside the Girls' Department, worked well. Each area had practices from 3.30pm-4.30pm, 4.30pm-5.30pm and 5.30pm-6.30pm: matches had to be arranged too, both indoor and outdoor. Where possible, we tried to accommodate the non-P.E. staff with first practices. I must say how blessed both departments were with these staff who willingly gave up their free time to help us out and take and coach teams. Such a large department had become necessary as the school approached 1500 pupils, and because of its size, the school eventually gained many successes against neighbourhood schools. Without being complacent, it was very satisfying to know that we were achieving such good results. After school practices now involved so many pupils that, at one stage, over 70% of the pupils attended at least one practice per week, and no pupil was ever barred from participating. That was as long as he or she had not incurred the wrath of any member of staff, and for many years therefore, despite the area the school was in, the school's discipline was good.

The standard of discipline in the two P.E. departments was very high and in the Seventies and Eighties easy to maintain. The large number of teams participating each night and the knock-on effect this had in maintaining discipline in class, was one hell of an asset for the P.E. staff and of course, the school. Those pupils who were not enthusiastic for P.E. at first, were not forgotten or missed out, and by cajoling them and using bulls--t, we tried hard to involve them in other fields of P.E. The scorers, timekeepers, kit men, 'secretaries', bell ringers etc generally came from this bunch of pupils. It was also a good way of keeping them interested in the lessons too.

It would be foolish to forget the fun we had in the department and I know that it was recognised by the pupils that we were not just nasty disciplinarians, but were also capable of having a laugh. If the fields were out of commission in the middle of winter; and they very often were as a result of pathetic drainage, then the Sports Hall was a boon. If a whole Year was on Games or P.E. well over a hundred boys or girls could be accommodated in the Sports Hall. Playing 5-aside football was not an option with those numbers, so we had a wet weather programme that kicked in which involved over half of the pupils being active for ten or fifteen minutes each, before we changed over the groupings to bring the others into play. Just occasionally, the staff would have a bit of fun and go back in time and teach counter-marching. Remember that? Moving round the sports hall in single line, coming down the middle and splitting both ways, the first pupil to the left, and the second to the right, going round the edge of the sports hall, but in the same direction, only to join together again at the bottom end of the sports hall and so on and so on until we had the biggest single line of pupils across the room, all coming down the middle together!

The fun, self discipline and concentration needed to perform this exercise was not to be sniffed at! Variations included 'shuffling' around, making a limping-walk and jogging around, all designed to increase thinking, and of course, fun.

The boy's P.E. Staff often led classes into lunch after lessons had finished like the Pied Piper. Dafter things like covering our mouths with a sticking plaster, a la Bernard Matthew's turkey advert, and then peeling the corner of the plaster back and growling "Norfolk" to the dinner ladies, just to wind the kids up. We might walk with an exaggerated limp, or a hop, into the dining hall with the kids in a line behind us copying our every move – all this nonsense, of course, helped to build up discipline and teamwork for the department. The younger kids thought we were barmy and thought we should have been sectioned! The senior pupils KNEW we were mad and often commented on this fact when they passed us on their way home for lunch.

'It must be nearly Xmas, they're at it again' they would say, having 'suffered' it in years gone by. Any daft ploy involving the staff and /or pupils was fair game for our 'survival' and the kids responded positively. Well at least they kept coming back to the department after school, in large numbers, and we were happy with that.

At Whitsuntide 1974 the new Head, Mr Gibbons, having taken over from the lovely Miss Evans, summoned me to his office and asked me to take on the post of Head of Year to the new Fifth Year. This was a big promotion I accepted the following day, despite wanting to snap his hand off there and then, but also involved keeping on the PE department. A challenge, yes, but also for me a move in the right direction and of course the extra money would come in handy now that Avril and I had another mouth to feed, our new daughter Anna. At home we were having great difficulties in coping with the news that our son Andrew was not a 'lazy boy' whose development was delayed, but was severely brain-damaged. This shock news would provide challenges unknown to us at that time. In 1981 I was promoted again to the post of Head of Upper School and my PE duties terminated, Andy Stewart becoming Head of Boy's P.E.

But for now, in the Seventies, the department was flourishing and my own duties expanded with my new post. Year Tutor duties included taking and organising Assemblies for up to three hundred pupils and staff first thing before school started in the morning. Occasionally I took my children into assembly with me which, in front of three hundred pupils, must have been daunting, but they coped. The job also included checking registers for pupil truancy and forged notes for absences, often with parental backing and compliance; having to meet regularly with the Educational Welfare Officer over a variety of issues and of course meeting many more parents in a totally different capacity from P.E. business. All part of the new direction I was taking in personal development as combined Head of Year and Head of P.E. and wondering where I might end up educationally having started as a P.E. assistant all those years ago.

Other involvement was to include organising the school Discos with Miss Hastings' brother Carlo on a monthly basis and running Sport's Nights in the PE Block for the Fifth Years most Wednesdays. The latter was a useful method of taking the older kids off the streets for at least one night a week and they always seemed to enjoy themselves. The activities further improved relationships between pupils and staff, and because of this, the staff support for these activities was surged and was really good on both of these nights. This was probably because most of the staff went for a much appreciated drink at a local pub afterwards! The sports evenings were far more relaxed than the school lessons with the exception of swimming, when pupils wore costumes and were always accompanied by staff for obvious safety reasons. No change of clothes necessary elsewhere, just casual clothes and clean trainers and that appealed more to the older pupils who flocked to the two activities and loved them: some called it 'Sports Night with Gordon.' In fairness it was so successful and something so necessary in the area that we continued running it long after I retired from teaching PE, with the support of the pupils, parents and staff.

We had some fabulous pupils in school that went on progressed and developed their personal physical skills to a high level in their own disciplines. In boxing, though not taught in school, we had Antonio who as an amateur, before turning professional, always had a group of staff to cheer him on at his fights. John and Andrew both played professional football for Luton Town and Birmingham City respectively. John was, I believe, the youngest player to play for Luton whilst still at school. Antony, who now lives in Australia, eventually went on to play for a Northern Ireland representative football side. His father, also Tony, was so proud when he brought his first 'cap' into school to show me, we were both in tears. Then there was six foot eight inches of 'Maggie' who went on and played cricket for Warwickshire, having first tried to break my ribs in the sports hall after school during practice. Elvis and Vincent both played first class basketball in Birmingham, but appeared to be back in school as much then as when they were supposed to have attended in the first place. Linda, Malcolm, Lesley and Sandra bounced and took part in trampoline displays in the Midlands, their hard work and dedication to their sport won them many competitions and plaudits along the way. Adrian was a superb high jumper and all-round athlete, a regular at the county championships and with Birchfield Harriers. Finally for now, Carl, Robbo, Chris, Andy and Percy who seemed to have flippers for feet as they swam through more water than anyone during my time in the PE department on their way to all the top Survival Awards.

The pupils I have mentioned were only the tip of a very large iceberg of excellence. Their achievements were obviously down to the skills they were born with and developed themselves and with encouragement from home, and using the facilities we could offer at school or recommend elsewhere. There were many pupils at school who could, and should, have achieved more. That they did not may have been because of any one or more key factors. It could have been down to me, or a lack of support from home, or that they did not have sufficient inner drive to develop further their undoubted talents despite them often being very capable of representing school and district-level teams. I can think of one young man who epitomised that thinking. He was a member of a very successful football side which I coached after I had finished teaching PE full time. He also became the lynch pin, and engine room, of the District side that achieved so much in his fifth year. Talking to him and his family, keeping everything above board, I arranged for him to go for trials with Leeds United, all expenses paid. Did he go? No way, not after he fell in love with a young lady. He then took a menial job and settled for a different style life when I think he could have done many times better. My observations I know, but of all those I taught and coached, he easily stood shoulder to shoulder with the best of them. Another pupil, who had real potential, finished what should have been a flourishing football career at a high level, by changing his football boots, at half-time, with one of his own team. Les was playing an absolute blinder in a District game in Stourbridge on an icy pitch, and made the swap in the dressing room at half time, changing rubber soled boots (perfect for the conditions) for a pair of nylon studded boots more suited to Torvill and Dean. Making his first challenge and tackle after the break, he fell over and badly dislocated his shoulder, which I understand, gave him constant and recurring trouble after he left school. He had the best close control of any footballer, a terrific change of pace off both feet, and that one mad impulse appeared to end a promising career in the game. How sad.

I said previously that it was not hard for us to 'sell' PE in the school because the vast majority of pupils were so keen to participate. The efforts of the PE staff in

Hey Teacher, You're 'aving a Larf

lesson time, the long hours of after school practices and out-of-school activities certainly helped. We coached two soccer teams in every year, sometimes three; cricket teams in every year; trampoline display teams; basketball teams in Years three, four and five; swimming teams in all years; inter-league school athletics teams in all years; badminton teams; cross-country teams in all years; and ran after school practices, as I described earlier, for all these teams. The department was very busy and I know the pupils appreciated our commitment.

Another side of PE was the wide range of outdoor activities we could offer. A trip to the school cottage in Wales, skiing abroad or on any of the artificial ski slopes nearby, Duke of Edinburgh Award expeditions, school camps in the Lake District or the Isle of Arran, trips to the Black Forest or 24 hour basketball events were not only all hugely beneficial to the children, but also gave the staff a different experience of the pupils outside of school. The constraints of the classroom, though very necessary, cannot always give the whole-child picture. When staff and pupils are out of the classroom environment, and in another completely different situation, any problems they may have with each other can often dissipate. The school's outdoor activities sessions were examples of this, and my only regret is that more staff and pupils were not able to participate.

Take for example the school cottage, Penyguelan, in the Hafren Forest in mid Wales. Not only was it close to the Clewedog Dam, made famous by a Land Rover advert, but the cottage was close to Plynlimon, the mountain which was the source of both the rivers

Severn and Wye. These trips to the cottage nearly always featured treks up Plynlimon, or for older pupils, Cader Idris. Those longer treks were designed to tire out all those pupils who liked to talk until the early hours of the morning whilst staff tried to sleep! Many were the times me and Andy were awakened by pupils at two or three o'clock in the morning and so we arranged a six thirty am breakfast, followed by a fifteen mile walk for them. Returning to the cottage and seeing big strapping athletes, at five o'clock on a Saturday evening, begging to go to their bedrooms upstairs for a kip, meant the walk achieved its aim. We, meaning I, would then prepare a 'spag bol' for the kids' dinner for when they woke up, whilst Andy pretended to prepare the following day's activities poring over O S maps. The kids insisted it was their favourite meal so we indulged their wishes: they had no choice! A highlight of the trip on a Saturday, if they were still awake, was the trip to the Star Inn at Staylittle, a former flourishing mining village. Now only populated by farmers and sheep, this formerly active and valuable village once had a population of over seven thousand people. Back in the pub, with written permission from their parents, the pupils were allowed no more than two pints. The kids never let us down on these occasions and always impressed the landlord, who had no idea of the pupil's backgrounds. However, the real highlight of the trips, for me at least, was setting up a night orienteering course and seeing the kids take part. Never more than four hundred yards from the cottage and with a partner, a torch and dressed in waterproofs, the pupils were given a route and had to collect clues for points, and we all know what points make. Pupils were always safely within sight of the cottage and its lights when they were out in the forest. It always surprised them how amazed they were by the eerie forest silence broken only by the call of a not-so-distant owl, or the continuous flowing water in the drainage ditches trickling to a larger stream. The experience of being in total darkness in the forest, stumbling over fallen branches, falling into drainage ditches and getting wet, was an experience they would not forget in a hurry. In my own case, following a visit to the Star Inn with Stew Cooper and returning to the cottage to layout the night's course, slipping and sliding, falling head over heels into a small ravine and becoming covered from head to toe in mud and sheep muck was also part of the staff experience too! Staff were trodden on and walked over, cursed black and blue, by the girls too, as we staff hid on the forest floor undetected. We knew the pupils enjoyed themselves because of the names they called us, not knowing we were close to them as they blundered around looking for clues. Most names would have made a Liverpool fish wife blush! The only dissent I can remember having from pupils was at the end of the trip. Someone had to empty the Elsan loos! Kids from Birmingham had never seen Elsan Blue toilets, and ooh, watching them digging the pit ......

As soon as he arrived at Smiths Wood, Andy Stewart began organising a Whitsuntide school camp, on the Isle of Arran, for Third and Fifth Year pupils. In 1982 I took Avril and Anna, who was nearly eight at the time. Goat Fell, beach walks, Lamlash, Brodick, the setting sun at the back of Lochranza, and the weather, were all sensational that week for all of us campers. I have many memories of that time: the sunsets; the 'flags' or yellow iris near Corrie that seemed to stretch for miles; the many basking sharks in Brodick Bay that caused panic all-round on boat trips; my mate Tony Harrison, in the corner of the bar in the Corrie Arms with his beloved glass of Glen Farclas whisky, each and everyone made that trip very special that year.

With a tiny little help from me, Andy Stewart, organised and set up a school summer camp in Torver, near Coniston in the Lake District. This always took place during the last week of term and the first week of the school holidays. We had reconnoitred a site at Tranearth, part way up the 'Old Man' of Coniston, and arranged a variety of pursuits and activities that were to be experienced by both staff and pupils during their stay. We also conducted training weekends for staff, prior to the pupils setting foot in camp. The training weekends with staff were almost as good as the camp weeks. Totally knackering though they were, we had so much fun that we almost forgot what their purpose was. Roger Airey was well known, after a few bevies, for pretending to look and act like a marine commando on exercise, but for one big difference: the darkened parts of his face were supplied by yours truly, acting as a make-up man, using donations left by sheep! No wonder he often sat alone after that, as the smell of what he had on his face did not make him popular with friends.

Andy Stewart, though an incredibly competent mountaineer, was never popular on, or after, these training weekends with staff. His habit of arranging

Hey Teacher, You're 'aving a Larf

marathon walks in the pouring rain up and around the 'Old Man' of Coniston in the dark, after a long journey up the M6 after a full day teaching at school, was well known. That would be followed by a night spent 'sleeping' in a roofless bothy, on a slope, which just so happened to have a stream flowing right through its centre where the carpet should have been positioned. With the slog of the all-day expedition that followed, a sleepless night was quietly forgotten as we discussed the merits of Lakeland Walks, in a bar of course.

Camp weeks took place with upwards of thirty pupils, accompanied by four or five extra staff, travelling from Birmingham to Windermere by train on the Monday morning of their week's camp. Brought by coach, on the last leg of their journey, they would arrive in camp for lunch. Expeditions over night somewhere close to the Old Man of Coniston, rock climbing, orienteering, canoeing, horse-riding in a beautiful part of the country, and showing respect and appreciation for that countryside, were very high on the agenda. Washing in the stream, cooking in a large mess tent for other groups not just their own, soon brought a spirit of camaraderie that lasted not only long after the week had ended, but well after they had finished and left school. The nights in camp, and certainly always the last Friday night, brought out the best, and loudest, singing in the mess tent. Games played, contests undertaken and the week's gossip and stories were recounted as they sat munching their burgers. It was not unusual to see tears shed, because they were returning home, on these occasions, perhaps, meaning the week had been successful. A system of camp commandments that we had introduced was regularly referred to during the course of the week. The commandment referred to most often was the 'Number 9,' or the 'Aesthetics' commandment. This involved the appreciation of beauty in general, but particularly the views of the Lakes and mountains, and pointing out to pupils *why* the Lakes were beautiful. How else would we, or they, have understood beauty had it not been explained to them?   One magical moment of country life I experienced during a night's camp in the hills, was with Una Duffy (Simpson) and Karen Downes, and a full expedition party of kids present in the camp, of course. Setting up the overnight camp that first sunny evening, we were interrupted by a gentleman running past us towing a cloth dowsed in aniseed. That single incident itself remains fixed in my memory. The man was followed several minutes later by a pack of hounds and, several minutes behind the main pack, a 'straggler', a dog that was for the kids, the star of the show. The surprise of seeing this country pursuit taking place was exciting enough, and the memory of the 'straggler' just brilliant, as he huffed and puffed along trying to catch up with his friends.

We had so many laughs with the pupils as we ploughed through the week's activities, and these were added to when things went wrong for staff. One of the funniest I witnessed, in all my years of involvement with the camp, was so hilarious it is difficult to describe, and involved Stewart Cooper and a huge horse. Careful! One activity was horse-riding and all pupils and staff experienced this, visiting stables near the beautiful Tarn Hows not too far from our main camp. Beautiful that

Hey Teacher, You're 'aving a Larf

is, if you were not Stewart Cooper. On the day in question, the group for horse-riding was divided into two smaller groups of about six pupils, and a member of staff accompanied each division. On this occasion it was Chris Burton and I, plus six pupils who eventually trotted out of the stables first and onto the trails in the forest nearby. Complete with riding hats, crops and an instructor, we had left the stables in an orderly line, just as one would have hoped for, despite me being on a horse that was twice as big as the others. There were no problems, no ill discipline by horse, pupil or staff, and forty five minutes later after a lovely trip, we re-entered the stables in an orderly line and dismounted our horses. The second group took over our horses and apart from Mr Cooper's hat that resembled Benito Mussollini's, all appeared to be going well as the line of horses left the stables again in an orderly line, except for one. This was the huge horse that seemed to pitch little Mr Cooper half way up to the clouds as it moved off. The horse then changed its mind and no longer followed the script. It carried on around the wall ignoring nudges and knee prodding from Stewart, taking no notice of any pull on the reins, and passed on the other side of the wall making back towards the stables. All we could see was Mr Cooper's head complete with helmet, bouncing along on the horse, his shoulders level with the top of the wall. Having expected to follow the line of the other horses, Mr Cooper looked to see where they were headed, only to find his horse leading straight back into the stables, with 'jockey' looking in the wrong direction. To say the horse's jockey looked surprised was an understatement and the look on his face said everything. We who were watching this episode in the mini bus were wetting ourselves with laughter, whilst the bus rocked violently. Upon leaving the stables again and being reunited with his group, Mr Cooper relaxed a little and managed a wry smile in anticipation of the trip going right from then on, and he went on his way with the others. Watching with anticipation for a repeat performance when the second group returned back to the stables, we in the mini bus were to be disappointed. However, all the way back to camp the mini bus was perpetually steaming up as Mr Cooper and Mrs Burton continued to recall the incident, over and over again.

Not content with his 'mania' for camping and their experiences, I let Mr Stewart sweet-talk me into participating in the Fourteen Peaks' walk in Wales. This involved walking and climbing all the peaks in Wales that are over three thousand feet high. Aaagh, I can still remember the state of my feet at the end of that day! With three staff and two fifth year pupils in our assault party, we set off on what was to be the hottest day of the year! A big support party helped and assisted our passage providing food and drink at pre-arranged stops. At the end of that day I was totally 'done in' but can well remember the confounded mountain in Snowdonia called Y-Garn. Anyone who has traipsed this route will need no explanation. My language that day did not appear in any English Language examination paper that summer! I was so sore as I fell into bed that night.

John Price, my deputy in the boys' PE department, spent many hours after school successfully training pupils to high levels of performance at trampolining. Those pupils gained medals in all competitions, both locally and at county level. I think, however, 'Pricey' preferred the weekend fetes and carnivals where his teams put on displays, enabling the pupils, and he, to demonstrate their amazing and complicated routines for the general public. For him it was a better way of selling the sport that he so excelled at himself. Even now, when he is supposed to be retired, he still holds training sessions for the sons and daughters of his former protégés and he remains a top class national judge at the sport too.

When we first had the indoor P.E. facilities I made sure he had the second senior school basketball team up until they left school. This was a talented team and because 'Pricey' loved his basketball and taught many of these pupils in PE lessons, it was simply better for continuity. They certainly loved him and made the school proud as they clawed their way up the best inter-school basketball leagues in Birmingham: the names of Elvis, Vince, Hugh, Donovan and Derek are but a few of the pupils that were under his wing. Pricey later organised two very successful 24 hour basketball sponsored events for school fund, with this team raising a considerable amount of money. He also formed the nucleus of his adult basketball team in the West Midland leagues using these pupils that at one stage also included the three aging male PE staff alongside the ex-pupils.

A main aim of a P.E. department must be to encourage pupils to continue their sports after they have left school, and the 'Old Boys' football teams and young cricketers being encouraged to join local club sides, assisted this objective. All that has to start somewhere and, for some budding gymnasts, this next little chestnut might have helped them decide otherwise. I well remember that first gymnastics lesson in the new and pristine gymnasium which involved using some brand spanking new gymnastic equipment. It was a Tuesday afternoon, straight after dinner and the 'gymnasts' were a Second Year boy's group. At this point I must make it clear to the reader, possibly recalling their own experiences of a first lesson in their school Gym, that the establishment of good routines was, and still is, an absolute priority for good practice in later years. In other words 'Thou shalt do it my way and no other' - a mantra so critical to avoid problems later. Boring though it is lifting mats out of the store cupboard is so important it has to be practised over and over until the exercise is perfect. Likewise, the same later, with the more 'exciting' equipment the pupils would eventually graduate to use. That is how it had always been in my experience, and that was the way it would remain here in the new gym. The lesson in question was proceeding fine as we established the correct routine for taking the mats out of the Gym's storage area. One person on the corner of each mat, 'Lift' and then 'Move' to the designated area of the Gym. 'Sit on your mats'. The pupils were not allowed to talk as they sat waiting patiently for the other groups to collect their new pristine mats. All boys were asked to observe each group of four collect their mat whilst remembering to look for 'good practice.' The mats in question were top of the range, water resistant, Nissen mats which cost the earth in 1973 and were going to have to last a long, long time. When all the mats were out and the class had warmed

Hey Teacher, You're 'aving a Larf

up by playing a small game, we came to the main theme of the afternoon: balancing in various ways on one's hands. This gymnastic task would hopefully lead them to perform a perfect hand-stand if they mastered some good balances. Pointing out good examples of pupils' work and asking the would-be gymnasts to demonstrate their sometimes astonishing, balances, and offering lots of praise and encouragement throughout the lesson, it was soon time for the class to return the mats, correctly, to the storage area.

'Sit, don't talk and watch the other groups put away their mats!' I bellowed.

'Good, well done that group! Next'

'Sit down boy.'

'But sir?' he persisted.

'I said sit down and wait your turn!'

'But sir, it's him sir' said the boy still pleading with me, 'Look sir!'

And there right in the middle of one of the new, water resistant, Nissen mats, three of the group having moved away from the offending area, one of the young 'gymnasts' had been overawed by the occasion and peed in the middle of the bloody mat! After such a good start to the proceedings, I could not bring myself to tell the little lad off, only encourage him next time, and of course keep a mop handy.

Our Physical Education equipment was expensive and had to be treated with absolute care to make it last. Just now and then, someone inside school, or a 'visitor', appreciated its value too, and removed it from the department, despite what we thought were good and secure safety regulations being in place. The pupils 'guarded' the stock carefully and it was checked in and out every lesson. One such theft involved the removal of six brand new Mitre Multiplex, full size, and very expensive footballs, taken when Night School was in progress. The following morning, when the P.E. teachers discovered the theft, we informed as many of the football team players as possible, knowing full well they would do our detective work for us. Sure enough, by lunchtime, the balls had been returned to their place in the storeroom, apparently returned by the 'thief' himself. Nothing was said and the crime did not occur again. The point I make is this: at that time the pupils took their sport very seriously, girls and boys, so woe betide anyone who risked spoiling their P.E. lessons. It was a good time to be teaching P.E.

I have mentioned how, in the Sports Hall, we used to occupy large numbers of pupils in counter marching when the weather was inclement. But it was also ideal for 5-aside football, basketball, netball, badminton, and any other game you care to mention; time and space would always be found for them. However, for me the Swimming Pool was my favourite place to teach, not because I was a good swimmer, far from it, but, by teaching a pupil to swim, you might equip them to save a life, perhaps their own. I well remember a pupil, named Alan, who had never been to a pool in his life let alone swum in one, being conned by me in his first lesson. First of all he used a float to support his body. He then thrashed his arms and legs about, holding the float, until he could move round the shallow end without it. Eventually, I asked him to walk and/or bounce on two feet, through to the deep end so he could feel the

Hey Teacher, You're 'aving a Larf

floating sensation, and that did the trick. Now more confident, he went on to swim a full length of the pool, with me bellowing at him of course. OK it was not pretty, but he was made a fuss of in his next Assembly and a couple of years later went on to represent the school at swimming when he was in the Third Year. He never forgot his moment. We used this 'procedure' regularly in the Pool and many pupils were able to start swimming after only a short spell with floats. You knew you were getting through to the pupils when the pool became quieter, not because of their lack of talking, but because of their better technique. One afternoon, on the poolside, I listened to Derby County's first foray into European football under Brian Clough on the school radio. I was able to hear the commentary because of the good technique of the 'co-operative' swimmers that lesson. Well that's what I told them.

For more able swimmers, the ASA Personal Survival Awards were a perfect way to stimulate pupils and the school's record as the pupils achieved these was excellent. So many pupils gained these awards right through to Honours from the Bronze award it became a real stimulus to do well.

The surrounding housing estate was a fervent football-loving area and so, when the school first opened, I was determined that the boys would play football as their main winter sport. Rugby would be introduced later, but to establish ourselves initially, we played football. We were not disappointed and were soon very successful at inter-school level, and with inter-class games which became a very strong feature of after school activities at certain times of the year.

The school went on to win several all-Birmingham trophies: the Trevor Gill Trophy with Kenny Taylor as manager, the Villa Cup and Blues Cup with Andy Stewart as manager, and the Blues Cup, on several occasions, with me, Wally Wowczuk as managers. This often gave our Washwood Heath colleagues, Tony Bishop and Pete Mortiboys who organised the Blues Cup competition, higher blood pressure than was healthy! Schoolboy league football certainly benefited the representative sides - Erdington and Saltley, and later the Solihull Schools F.A., and provided the pupils with the opportunity to excel. League games against Kim White's Castle Vale, Washwood Heath, Graham Smallburn's Stockland Green and Mervyn Parsons' Whitesmore teams all provided those District sides with quality footballers. I really believe that even with all the football played in the Birmingham area in those days at school, or on Sundays, pupils and staff enjoyed District Schools' representation and do so to this day.

In the summer despite the shortened term and the longer holiday, we always felt that despite the efforts of P.E. staff in all schools, we were never fully able to do justice to the summer sports of athletics, cricket and tennis. Coaching athletic field events, the forward defensive stroke in cricket or the overhead smash in tennis on a bitterly cold May morning at nine thirty am, was not going to produce world beaters in the UK from school playing fields. The early rounds of District athletics, always sadly occurred before any meaningful practice of the discus, shot or javelin had been conducted in the athletics' coaching programme for First Years in particular, but other years too. Outdoor grass facilities

Hey Teacher, You're 'aving a Larf

for cricket in state schools seemed to deteriorate nationally at the same time as our own international England teams declined in quality. Try as we might in the UK at summer sports, we will never be able to compete and punch our weight alongside those countries that have far more favourable weather conditions. Australia, South Africa and Spain are examples of countries with smaller populations that punch above their weight in tennis, swimming, athletics and with the two Commonwealth countries, cricket. Perhaps we should build larger indoor sports facilities that have gigantic retractable roofs: fully-roofed stadiums may be the way to achieve success. The ever-escalating cost of presenting the Olympic Games is a worry for me, not only because politicians can never be relied upon to stick to their original cost estimates, but also because I do not think we are able to compete at the highest level in sport anymore. Why? Firstly, our facilities are not up to scratch. Secondly, our schools are losing too many playing fields as authorities sell them off. Thirdly, our participation levels in all sports are not high enough per head of population when compared to the rest of the world. Lastly, the children today that are interested in sport have too many distractions to persuade them away from their chosen sport. But we shall soon see in the 2012 London Olympic Games what price any medals we may win have cost us.

I have alluded to the fact that the British weather was not all that we would have hoped for during preparations for, and the playing of, outdoor sports. That was certainly the case in winter, especially on our poorly drained football pitches at Smiths Wood. The weather conditions seldom prevented us though from coaching outside, except on the rare occasions when there were heavy snowfalls, or constant heavy rain flooded the already saturated fields. When I look back and consider how badly those fields drained, it is a credit to the pupils and their enthusiasm, that the drop-out rate in lessons was almost non-existent. Motivating the pupils was never a problem. We tried hard to maintain a high personal contact level with footballs, basketballs and rugby balls, often with a ball each, and always at least one between two. We felt the more time 'on the ball' the quicker and better the personal skill of the pupil would develop. Maintaining this aim, in all sports, was made easier because we were supported with generous capitation allowances.

I mentioned that motivation was not always needed in this sports-mad area, and nowhere was this truer than in some of the fifth form games lessons which became battles, not only between the pupils, but also between the staff. Attempting to 'psych' out the opposing team, and its member of staff, began to take on unprecedented levels of competition. Simply lining up before the start of the game and saluting an imaginary crowd, 'a la Leeds United' or appearing in team shirts, not bibs or vests, or even serving slices of orange at half-time, all served to 'up the ante'. The kids loved it, the staff enjoyed it and apart from absence from school, not one pupil missed one of these games lessons. Nowadays, when I meet and greet old boys and reminisce about the 'good old days,' usually over a pint, those games always crop up somewhere in the conversation.

Hey Teacher, You're 'aving a Larf

The good banter and competition between the PE staff often left the boys with their mouths wide open, as the contests between 'Pricey', Andy and me, and eventually Kenny, did not stop at just football. Basketball shooting practice, table-tennis, badminton, cricket, swimming, tennis, athletics, in fact anything that involved a moving ball or shuttle-cock, always involved a challenge between staff! Most of it was just hot air and designed to increase the personal competition between pupils. Pupils always noticed though that we never challenged 'Pricey' on the trampoline or in the gym though, not when he had represented his country at Gymnastics!

Staff matches, versus the pupils, came and went, but I vividly remember the very first staff versus pupil's football match, way back in 1975. Most of the staff team were still under thirty years of age, quite fit, and skilful enough to play sport and turn a trick except for one rotund Science teacher. Although an avid fan of the game, he would probably have been better as a spectator, but then we were short of players that day. During the game, both sides enjoyed the usual banter with each other, but I distinctly remember hearing two lads in the pupils' team taking the mickey out of 'Mr Rotund'. Interrupting, I informed them that, in his youth, he had been for trials with Birmingham City. The looks on their faces told me they thought I was talking rubbish, until at that very moment 'Mr Rotund' unleashed a vicious and dipping shot from all of thirty yards that smashed into the crossbar and flew out for a goal kick. After that, 'Mr Rotund' was a hero and I thanked God that his shot came at that moment and saved my blushes.

As the department increased in size so did the number of representative teams and the range of after-school activities. That brought with it the demand for more staff to assist with the coaching and managing of those teams. Bob Cherrington, for example, ran every first year football side whilst he taught at Smiths Wood, which made all our lives much easier in the department as he sorted out the new intake. Many of these staff played on Friday nights in a local 5 a-side football league. The teams were mainly from staff working in local schools who often socialised together afterwards in the local hostelries. Smiths Wood were very fortunate at the time with staff that could play, or thought they could play, and so were able to field three 5 a-side teams in the Seventies and Eighties using thirty staff some nights which needed a very careful substitute system devised by concerned members of staff. The prime mover in this staff 5-a-side scheme was Steve Hasnip who had run one of the schoolboy teams for me and who seemed to be available to play in every 5-aside game going! His enthusiasm for his Friday night kick-about never waned, even when Andy Stewart suffered a broken leg in a 5-aside staff game. Steve was overheard asking, in a casual way, 'How long will it be before we can carry on?' That's the official version anyhow!

One bonus of teaching PE was the chance to arrange skiing trips and so it was no surprise when Stewart Cooper, Val Pickard (Long) Head of Girls' P.E. and I organised the first trip to the Austrian ski slopes of Pertisau, for Easter 1973. All arrangements appeared to be in order the night before our departure, as I systematically and repeatedly checked over and over again the collective passport, pocket money, itinerary etc. etc. The following day was a normal school day, prior to departure and our night flight from Luton Airport: everyone was looking forward excitedly to the trip. Stewart and Val were taking their other halves, but, sadly, I was not able to take Avril now that Andrew was a year old.

Arriving at school on the morning of the trip all seemed normal until I entered the main P.E. block and found a very distressed Val waiting to talk to me. She told me her husband Roger had a morbid fear of flying which had deteriorated so badly overnight that he felt unable to fly that evening. It looked as if the trip would have to be cancelled. Over my dead body it would. Finding Val's husband very distressed, alone in his car, in a school car park, I was able to 'express my feelings' to him even at that late hour. Thus we travelled to Luton by coach as arranged, flew to Munich and transferred to our resort with a full compliment of staff and pupils. A few words of 'help' and a swig of whisky can be a remedy for problems at times: they certainly were in that instance. Austria was to become too expensive for future skiing holidays and so the next skiing trip, in 1975, was to Italy.

The first trip there was memorable for several reasons, particularly the enthusiasm shown by the pupils for skiing. That meant we needed far more staff to help run and supervise the pupils on the second trip to Misurina in Italy. One excellent athlete and footballer gave me cause for concern as he had not paid for his trip by the deadline set. Although I asked him over and over again for the balance of payment, his reply was always 'It will be alright sir'. It was, the money arrived before we left for Italy and 'Albert' went on the trip, had a fantastic time and was skiing quite proficiently by the end of the week as we knew he would. However, several months afterwards, it transpired that his father was the 'banker' for a Post Office robbery in the Midlands and had spent the money whilst the gang were caught and jailed. Now they were out of jail and wanted the cash! And we had used some to pay for a skiing trip. OoooooH! Ouch!

The volume of snow that was present on this trip as we arrived in the resort, perched at 6000 feet above sea level, and the further snowfalls whilst we stayed there, were unbelievable. Margaret Butterfield, the senior lady member of staff on the trip, referred to the depth of the snow daily as we walked to the ski slopes. At the beginning of our stay we could see the whole of the village's tennis courts adjacent to our slopes and we were able to walk, with our skis, under red, white and blue plastic indicators of power lines. At the end of the week we could not see the tennis courts, and we stepped OVER the power lines! In all this, a certain 'Billy Whizz' as he was affectionately known by staff, taught Maths in school and, following personal problems, joined our party at the last moment for his first time on skis. Completely fearless, he developed a good technique on his skis and was soon taking to the ski lifts so he could experience the more challenging ski slopes. Whilst giving extra skiing instruction to some pupils one afternoon, me and the other staff and pupils turned to look up the mountain as a most thunderous noise originated from that direction. Suddenly, flying down and out at the bottom of the main slope, at a great rate of knots, appeared 'Billy Whizz' who snowploughed to a halt in front of me, totally out of breath, just as the noise on the mountainside died down. What he had done was outrun an avalanche somehow, and not surprisingly, was soon seen disappearing in the direction of the nearest toilet. Clearly, it continued to prey on his mind a great deal that evening, which is probably why we found him later locked between the two retaining doors to his room, and not in his bed!

A memorable visit to Venice rounded off our first trip to Italy before our flight home. The visit finished for Stewart Cooper and me after we ate horsemeat, in our goulash for lunch, and then, as we stepped outside our restaurant, proceeded to hurdle across and over the Grand Canal! Only joking, honestly!

Andalo and Monte Bondone, again both in Italy, were other trips on the skiing itinerary and apart from the second trip to Monte Bondone by coach and road, the other two had very good snow conditions. Not so the second visit to Monte Bondone, which was almost bereft of snow forcing us to travel a long way to ski each morning in another valley.

My final ski trip was unusual for me as both Avril and my daughter Anna came too, and Andy Stewart by now Head of Boy's P.E., organised the trip to Tauplitz in Austria in 1988. Staying in our hotel at the same time were officers of the Austrian Territorial Army and also based in the village were the soldiers in their Territorial Regiment. It was like walking into the set of a war film. The uniforms seemed to belong to a former age! Not being put off by this show of military strength, the trip was full of fun as Avril and Anna, on skis for the very first time not only struggled to ski but, watching them negotiate the T-bar and being dragged to the top of the nursery slope was so funny, I had difficulty staying on my own skis.

On the same holiday the generosity of one of the parents was totally unparalleled in my short experience of organising school skiing trips. Arriving after us at the same hotel, with his other two daughters, this Dad introduced himself to the school staff having parked his Daimler Sovereign! Arriving late on the Saturday morning, and after being allocated our rooms, we found, to our dismay, that the village shops were closed for the weekend. This meant that our pupils could only buy drinks (non-alcoholic) in the hotel and they were VERY expensive. Hearing of the kids' problem our knight in shining armour offered his services. He took himself off to the nearest supermarket, filled his car boot with fizzy drinks, and drove back to the hotel and just doled them out to our group, for free. This act of extreme generosity was without equal in my time at Smith's Wood. I can assure you that the young skiers from Birmingham were very, very grateful for this man's efforts. His import-export business must have been very profitable for him to be so generous.

It was only after we had arrived back home, and several months later when reading the local evening paper that I found an article that brought me rapidly to my senses. The 'shining knight' had been arrested in his hotel room in Stockholm, for……. dealing in cannabis.

Hey Teacher, You're 'aving a Larf

My final international trip was to the Black Forest in Germany riding 'shotgun', as the senior member of staff, with Mrs.Carol Pitt, Mr Steve Hasnip, Avril my wife, and John Whittingham. A happy trip, but we almost caused an international incident travelling back across the border as we left Germany. But first, the trip down from school to the Black Forest and two incidents I will never forget as long as I live.

We left school in a superb double-decker bus which had most of the passenger seats upstairs, where the kids sat. Downstairs another area contained a toilet and a separate section, with seats, that was used as a storage area for all the cans of pop and chocolate biscuits the drivers would sell to the kids. Staff escaped downstairs for peace and quiet away, not from the kids, but from the endless videos of music and films.

One minute there we were travelling along French motorways and, before we knew it we were on German autobahns. In Germany most of the autobahns are concrete based, and tyres continually rumble over them, unevenly. The ladies seemed to need to test the plumbing regularly on those roads! When Avril had to test the plumbing it was apparent, according to my good lady, that the road was extra bumpy and bendy at that time. 'It could only happen to me' has often been her moan when things went wrong, and this was to be no exception. Whilst in the toilet all of a sudden, and without warning, the bus careered round a tight bend, the toilet door flew open, and there, pulling up her trousers whilst flying out of the door, was Avril. She repeated the process, in reverse, as the bus swung the other way around another corner, and with Avril thrown back into the toilet, the door closed! By now beetroot red, embarrassed, and having lost all her feminine poise, she crept out of the loo to find Mrs Pitt doubled up in uncontrollable laughter.

More toilet humour for the reader? Discovering that the toilet was now 'full,' having been 'loaded' by an almost constant procession of pupils needing to try out the plumbing or perhaps, more relevant, to visit the scene of Avril's toilet incident, what could we do about the problem? Prevent the kids from using the loo? Stop on the autobahn every few minutes? No, just ask the driver, silly! In unison, the drivers said they would deal with the problem as soon as possible. Little did we realise that the release of the 'goods' would occur on a German road as the bus negotiated a very long and tight bend! Ugh!

This whole trip away was brilliant. The pupils, as they often were in these situations, were really well behaved and good fun to be with. The hotel accommodation was good, but the real treat was the food that was served up. The constant cries from the chef, in his pidgin English at the evening meal was, 'Do you like cheeeeps?' The reply each time from the kids was 'Yes we do, bring 'em on.' This delight and contentment with the food was not only confined to the kids. Oh no. When, on the first night, turkey legs were brought out on plates for all to see, the eyes of Herr Hasnip and Herr Whittingham were out on stalks, they could not believe their luck, or the size of the turkey legs. And when asked if they would like extra, guess whose hands were raised first? Correct, the two Herrs!

Hey Teacher, You're 'aving a Larf

The day's activities and trips out were well organised, with all pupils and staff taking part. After dinner, those who wished to, performed the nightly ritual of visiting the phone box in the village, whatever the weather, to phone home to keep up with progress in Coro', Emmerdale or 'Enders. (German Telecom must have made a fortune that week on calls to the UK from the Black Forest.) On the last night but one, the staff met in the bar for the usual 'briefing', and on this occasion, a quiet 'goodbye' drink. The following day would involve a day trip followed, on departure day, by an early start and so, sadly, this was our last drink in the hotel. In the company of the German locals we enjoyed good banter, exchanging football stories and the like, and as the night lengthened and the alcohol began to flow the music began. Soon we were singing our national songs in competition with the locals, smiling kindly towards our friendly hosts. Joint songs and anthems grew louder and louder until everyone had left the bar after midnight. At breakfast the next morning, several of the pupils stood aside and clapped us as we entered the dining hall for, as they said, 'beating the Germans at singing!'

For the homeward journey a list of pupil purchases was compiled, ready for the Customs Officers we would meet at the border crossings on the journey home. This meant no knives or anything sharp or illegal; no cigars, cigarettes or alcohol, or even miniature bottles for parents! Journeying home and about twenty miles from the border, on the way to Luxembourg, I happened to remind the kids of what had been said about presents, and, if they needed to, they should add things to the list now. Likewise, if they now felt something was dodgy and might be picked up on any x-ray machines at the border, they should put the item in the box provided, and I would show the Customs Officers when the time came. Much to-ing and fro-ing occurred on the bus at that moment, accompanied by the opening of bags, and five minutes later I peered casually into the box we had provided for dodgy items. There to my astonishment I saw an assortment of probably fifty or more condoms. Who for? 'My mum and dad' was the reply in all cases but one, which was a purchase for an elder brother! (Was sex education beginning to work in our school?) At the border crossing the unbelievably efficient Germans checked and double-checked the paper work involving the collective passport. BUT they did not want to check any pupils, but they did want to see ALL the staff who then disembarked from the bus with heads hung low, to be searched at the Customs. The kids loved it, absolutely loved it. If they had been able to write a script humiliating the staff at the end of the holiday, then this was it. For them this was a fitting end to a good holiday.

Being Head of Upper School was so different from working in the P.E. Department. There was no subject to sell and only pupils, parents and staff to interview, which mostly and sadly, involved indiscipline in pupils. This new post though important, could be very negative at times. There were, however, many positive times: it was good to praise individuals, teams and staff for their successes or achievements. The school had put on musicals, the Wizard of Oz being the first, which set the standard for all future musical achievements.

Hey Teacher, You're 'aving a Larf

Choirs, orchestras and steel bands all represented the school at functions throughout the West Midlands very successfully. Pantomimes, involving pupils and staff acting side by side, brought the school almost to a standstill when the rehearsals led up to the shows. They were so successful it was a sad day when they finished.

Taking and organising Assemblies could sometimes prove difficult with staff absence, particularly at a moment's notice, and at first, in my new role I was caught short, so to speak, several times. Most Assemblies had moved away from the religious Grammar School-type assemblies of my youth, to become more moralistic, and often more entertaining, usually with a powerful message. One that was a big surprise for the school involved a former school and college friend of mine, Brian Jones. Brian and I go back a long way and, in our respective sixth forms, we both played for Derbyshire Grammar Schools at football. During the time we played for the County we toured Manchester United's ground in the summer of 1963, and we were invited to look at, and hold, the recently won FA Cup. Brian was lifted up and sat on my shoulders, as if to celebrate winning. On being passed the cup and lid to hold aloft, he dropped the cup on the floor and yes slightly dented it. Mr Busby was not amused! Now here he was, in September 1982, with the manager of Aston Villa, Tony Barton, in the school theatre, holding aloft the European Cup recently won by the 'Villa' in Rotterdam on May 25th 1982. The Fourth Year pupils in the theatre that day will never forget that assembly as long as they live. I don't suppose the staff will forget those twenty five minutes and that Assembly either.

In a new school there are always new ideas. Many innovative ideas were tried and implemented when Smiths Wood School was first opened and growing in numbers. One innovation that caught the eye, and had its funny side, involved the Head, Mr Gibbons, long before the politicians got hold of his idea. This involved pupils having a breakfast in school before lessons. Come the first and big day with breakfast, local television and radio were buzzing about the school as the only pupil to arrive for breakfast did so as the cameras rolled. The pupil ate his breakfast, the Head gave his interview to the assembled media, and everything looked hunky dory. The pupil was also interviewed, and his opinions on and about his freshly-prepared bacon sandwich would have impressed Rick Stein. Here is the rub: the kid was never, ever in school before the bell went for registration at the start of the school day, and as soon as he had eaten his breakfast he ran off out of school again! The initiative soon died a death, becoming too expensive to run, but it was as they say, 'cool at the time of delivery'. Some dysfunctional pupils tried coming into school just to eat their dinner, even though they had truanted the morning's lessons, and would truant again in the afternoon! In fact, school just interfered with the lives of some pupils, full stop.

In the late Seventies and early Eighties there were up to 1500 pupils on roll aged from twelve to sixteen, and, in a school built for 1200. There were bound to be accidents on or off the premises, and tragically, some accidents would end in death. One pupil was killed on the crossing close to school and the effect the poor girl's death had on both pupils and staff was simply awful. Another accident which could have proved fatal, but thankfully did not, was reported in the local press. Just to say that the main reason for someone shouting the word 'Stop!' is maybe to ensure a person's safety and an immediate reaction to it may save a life. One young lady failed to do so as she ran out of school, after registration, one afternoon. She failed to adhere to, or hear, the call of 'Stop!' ran out of school and straight across the road, and was hit by a bus. She ran so fast, without looking to check for traffic on the road that the bus could not stop in time and so hit her. Miraculously for her, she was hardly bruised, let alone injured, but her leg was slightly trapped under a wheel of the bus. Pupils leaving school, passers-by on foot or in cars, all crowded round. Other staff responded to the noise of squealing of brakes and followed me and 'Pricey' out of school and began sorting out the traffic and the leering crowd. The male Deputy Head helped the driver to reverse slowly and release the girl's trapped leg and she was soon up and away home, after being inspected by several first-aiders. The following nights' press made interesting reading – 'Six amazingly strong teachers lift bus off girl's leg'. As if. But we did have a plate of spinach to plough through and eat in the staffroom next day after a kindly donation!

    That wasn't the only press headline that was exaggerated about the school. On another later occasion, a pupil in an altercation with another pupil, slightly injured him close to his eye. 'Pupil stabbed in eye', a headline in the paper that evening did nothing for the school's reputation and was totally untrue. But as we all know mud does stick. That was thick mud.

Being so large the school had many characters over the years that were to leave their mark on myself and others. There was the 'Nit Nurse' who always arrived following a 'sighting' as one would say. When she arrived in school every child had to have their hair checked with what appeared to be the same comb! In our first year, one family was notorious for acquiring nits and the 'Nit Nurse' seemed to be permanently at our school. The mere mention of that family name, even today, has my good friend Stewart Cooper, scratching himself all over. Stewart was involved in the next little gem, shortly after I had retired, but it makes me laugh each time it is recalled. As a Head of Year he was responsible for checking his Years' registers and acting accordingly, with or without the Welfare Officer, if he felt a pupil was truanting, or if an absence note did not make sense and a home visit was in order. That was the reason he was out of school on this occasion, or so the story goes. Coming across a former young lady pupil they exchanged the usual pleasantries and he asked her how things were with her and her family. She explained that all was fine and that her brother, who Stewart had taught during his time at school, had just 'come out'. At that precise moment there followed a problem interpreting what she said.

'Come out?' said Stewart, 'I didn't know he'd been in. What did he do? Where was he, Winson Green Prison?'

'No' replied the young lady, 'come out as in gay, you know gay, coming out. He's gay.' And with that answer, no stone was big enough to hide Stewart's embarrassment!

Hey Teacher, You're 'aving a Larf

A 'misunderstanding' of sorts, with a funny side to it, happened on the very first day Andy Stewart taught in the school. A pupil was irritating Andy, and the rest of the class, by constantly flicking his pencil in the air off the side of his desk, watching it fall onto the floor, and then, very slowly, picking it up. A cuff round the ear should have done the trick, shouldn't it? The bell went for the end of the lesson and the class was dismissed. At the end of the following lesson when the bell for Break had rung and Andy had dismissed his new class from the same classroom as before, he was walking along the corridor when a very irate and very large parent appeared in front of him. This parent was exceedingly angry that his little boy had been cuffed behind his ear. Enquiring as to where Mr Stewart taught, Andy pointed towards the classroom he had just left! The parent marched towards the room Mr Stewart hurrying in the opposite direction to report the incident to the Deputy Head. Apart from giving us all a laugh, even Andy later on, it was not something he ever repeated.

At school examination time internal examinations were held in the pupil's lesson time and 'covered' by the staff who should have been teaching the group that lesson. That is how I often found myself invigilating a group that would normally have been having P.E. Mischievously, if a pupil was absent from the exam, and to pass the time, I always filled in some dodgy answers on their paper. Being devilish, I would enter silly or deliberately wrong answers and slip the answer paper in with the others after the exam had finished. Listening to staff comment on pupils' ability as they recalled the answers on some exam papers made my exercise worth the effort. I just hope no pupil suffered because of my stupidity!

On a particular Science paper I really 'went to town' in the name of some poor youth who was absent that day. The class was the responsibility of 'Mr Rotund' the Science teacher, who, later on, was regaling the staff room with examples of answers from the paper. He almost ran through a box of tissues wiping the tears of laughter from his eyes, as we too laughed, because we could not believe he had fallen for such crass answers. Trying to tell him it was me who had written the answers was a complete waste of time as he would not listen! Ah well, it made some of us laugh at the time.

1981 was a particularly cold year, with heavy snowfalls and low temperatures breaking all previous winter records. One member of staff, 'W', caught up in that cold winter, was living in a caravan in a field. Daily, the staff room was buzzing as teachers told their do-or-die stories of journeys to and from school in Arctic conditions. But none could beat this anecdote. Asking 'W' how he was coping in the intense cold in his caravan, one member of staff was told:

'It was the coldest night of the winter by far last night. How do I know? Because, when I woke up this morning, even my hot water bottle was frozen between my legs!'

I cannot better that.

One necessary task that the Community nurses and doctors fulfilled was the inoculation of pupils against TB. All Third Year pupils reported to the Small Hall on these days, sent for by a member of staff, class by class. Assembling quietly they then progressed, in line, up the Admin Block stairs to the Medical Room to be injected. This was not a popular activity for pupils and was a long way from being their favourite pastime. Panic and fear could spread like wildfire if not stopped immediately, and could sometimes get out of hand. I know from both sides, as an organiser of the scheme, and also as a minion supervising the pupils in the queue, what could happen if the fear-factor got out of hand. One particular episode stands out above all the rest and occurred early in 1974. Two pupils of vastly different heights, one was six foot four inches and a big bully, the other four feet six inches and a good laugh, were the best of mates. The big one did not like needles of any size; the little one knew this and tormented his friend wickedly. If anyone else been involved the incident would never have happened. But it did ……. and how. The tormenting of the big one reached a quiet crescendo as his pallor changed from bright red to ashen, as the approaching 'needle time' got nearer. With one last teasing comment a few yards from the room's opening, the little one performed his *coup de grace*: the big one passed out and collapsed to the floor, eventually coming round in the Medical Room, just in time for his injection! 'Beam me up Scotty' took on a completely different meaning from that moment.

I have mentioned that a pastoral role in school could be quite negative, constantly dealing with discipline problems and the increasing amount of paperwork to keep records up to date. From a personal point of view, I knew of several friends who 'retired' from that very role in a number of schools, crushed by those burdens.

Lawrence Gordon

Many times, as I have tried to show in the last few paragraphs, there was also a funny side to being in the staffroom, the classroom or on games field, which lightened the load. Nevertheless, a side I personally had great difficulty dealing with was the death of a pupil, either by illness or accident. Increasingly, both in the pastoral role and in my former capacity as Head of PE, I was involved with many parents and I often became the first port of call when serious illness afflicted a pupil. How parents ever deal with the death a child I do not know and, God forbid, neither do I want to know. From experience, I know the parents' and families' anguish: their hurt and sense of loss is never diminished, despite the passage of time. Having attended the funerals of many pupils and having visited their homes during their illnesses, I can only begin to understand the trauma and the heartbreak.

On one occasion whilst visiting a pupil in hospital suffering from leukaemia, I heard someone talking in the room next door, asking if it was Mr Gordon's voice that they could hear. When I answered their question I discovered another former pupil in that room with a similar type of leukacmia. That set me thinking when I returned home. I have no proof, scientifically or medically, and it is just my own gut-feeling based upon my lengthy knowledge of the area, but what I think is this: draw a line about a mile in length through the school from the North West to the South East, and a couple of hundred yards wide. On each side of the line you will find, since 1978, many instances and varieties of cancer that have afflicted both pupils and staff. I can think of at least twenty deaths and illnesses during my

Hey Teacher, You're 'aving a Larf

time at Smiths Wood and that, surely, is not normal for one school.

By 1991 the school had shrunk in numbers, the Head of Lower School had retired and the then Head teacher, Mr Fox, asked me to assume responsibility for both Upper and Lower School. I thus became Director of Pastoral Care. That meant a widened brief and responsibility which I was happy to take on, develop and maintain, until my career was interrupted and finished through illness. In fairness it was little different from my previous role but included more contact with younger pupils. However, increasing problems at home with my severely brain damaged son Andrew, who rarely slept more than a couple of hours a night, finally helped take its toll on my health. I therefore had to leave my life and career in school if I wanted to stay alive and watch my children mature as adults.

Nevertheless Smith's Wood was to make one more lasting big impression on me, in a pastoral sort of way. A large group of thirty plus former pupils had heard that I had not had a proper retirement 'do', when I left school, because I had been so ill. So they set about arranging a meet in a local hostelry, when I was well enough to venture out again. This time also coincided with a serious assault on Andrew by a member of staff at the hospital unit he attended for respite. That night in question, while the beer was flowing, one of my former pupils sidled up alongside me and asked if I would tell him the name of the hospital worker who had assaulted my son. He had heard about the incident from another former pupil and promised me that, if I told him the name of the assailant, he would not harm him. He just wanted, he said, to have a word in 'that bastard's' ear. After all, he told me, if I had not intervened when he was a pupil and 'sorted him out' at school he would not have turned out as well as he had. Despite my refusal to give him the name of the person involved, and my reluctance to continue the conversation, he was persistent. Had he persisted as hard at school with his academic work, he might not have been sitting next to me at that moment, in the pub, pleading with me for information. Oh, and the main reason I refused to tell him the information he wanted? I thought I'd drop in the text here that he had just completed six years in jail for manslaughter having stabbed a man to death! Enough said on that. The same night the 'old boys' were wishing me well health-wise, a public house close to the school was raided by the police looking to make arrests because of drug dealing. The boys obviously knew they would be safer with me. Ha Ha bloody Ha!

Finally, two occurrences experienced in my pastoral role that were never mentioned in the job specs. The names are false of course. Following an interview with a mother late one Friday afternoon whose son had been in serious trouble and had been suspended from school for a while, she completely caught me unawares when, seemingly not concerned with her son's misdemeanours, said

'…. And my husband's left me for another woman, what am I going to do for sex this Friday night Mr Gordon?'

I hadn't realised until that moment what was meant by 'community support!'

Hey Teacher, You're 'aving a Larf

The last story concerns a young man who was regularly in trouble with the police. His mother sat before me, with thirty bob's worth of material wrapped round her and looking like Alice Cooper on a bad day. She was explaining about 'our bab's' problems. The interview went thus:

'So what has Sidney been up to now Mrs Blue, not enough for the police to pay another visit I hope?' I enquired politely.

'I just don't know what's got into him lately, Mr Gordon. There he was the other night, on the carpet in the middle of the lounge, giving his girlfriend one… he is forward, I know……. when the doorbell rang. I answered the door and it was his mate asking for Sidney. I said he was with his girlfriend, what did he want? He said to tell Sidney he'd nicked a car, and did he want to come for a joy ride? Hearing that, and without a word, our Sidney gets off his girl, zips himself up, and leaves the house. What's wrong with him Mr Gordon?'

What's wrong with him Mrs? Look in the mirror I say.

Summarising my time in teaching, I must say that teaching was my oxygen. I loved the job even when it became tough towards the end. And boy, did I have fun! So many happy moments and friendships made down the years, I find it hard to believe it was all crammed into my career. Sadly, my teaching career came to an untimely end, but at least I am still alive to tell the tale, which did not look likely back in 1995.

After School Activities

Having been involved in sports and outdoor activities all my life it came as a huge shock when a series of illnesses forced me to terminate my teaching career prematurely. My illnesses were, I suppose, brought about by sleep deprivation over many years and all its associated complications. With my sleep pattern increasingly disturbed it was not surprising that, sooner or later, something had to give and I would hit a 'brick wall'. Sadly, having taken my family to the limits of their patience during my illnesses, I am humbly grateful to them for sticking by me through those times.

Life was not all doom and gloom though away from the classroom even before, and since I retired. For example, not many people know I had been the role model for Frank Spencer in the TV series, 'Some

Mothers Do Have 'Em'. At least, that is what my family reckons when it comes to my attempts at DIY, and several examples help to illustrate my feeble attempts to decorate our home. I have really tried to overcome my incompetence at DIY but have to admit total failure in that discipline. An example of my hopelessness was my first attempt to decorate the kitchen. Stripping the paint from the window frames with a blow torch, I easily peeled away several layers as recommended by none other than Barry Bucknell, the 'do it yourself' TV man, whose TV house fell down. Eventually, I came across a mysterious pink layer that I found very hard to remove. When my wife asked me what I was doing, as by now I had burnt the frames and they were turning dark brown, I pivoted on the ladder to explain what I was up to and my blow torch set fire to two tea towels hanging on a rail a yard away. Smoke, fire, paint and expletives were filling the kitchen but, fortunately for me, little damage was done once the fire was doused! When the friendly joiner came to replace the back door leading to the garden from the kitchen, he inspected all the frames and said how sorry he was to see we had experienced a bad fire, and sympathetically enquired how it had started. When told, he fell out of the back door laughing his head off, I could have kicked him. But I would probably have missed him!

Wallpapering, now there's another skill that has by-passed me. Early in our marriage there was much decorating to be done and we often used wood-chip paper on the walls because it was cheap. When our main bedroom needed decorating and the kids were asleep one Sunday night, we started to assemble our materials. Paste brush, paste and bucket, decorating table, step-ladder, even a pair of scissors to cut the paper, the bedroom furniture covered in dust sheets……. all appeared to be in order. Avril passed the first piece of pasted paper to me…..I dropped it. Avril handed it back, I held it firmly, placed it in the correct position on the wall, so I thought, and began opening it out. I slid it around to fit into the correct position, tore some of it off, wrinkled some, put my hand through the soft wet paper, ripped it all off, screwed it up and threw it on the floor. I apologised to my wife, who patiently prepared another piece of wood-chip paper, and I stepped down to take it from her – in doing so, I trod on the wallpaper, not once but twice; first my left foot and then my right foot went straight through the paper. By now, Avril's eyes were popping out of her skull like half-pulled corks in a wine bottle as she tried desperately to hold back a giggle. Being the polite, kind, laid-back lady she is, she patiently cut and pasted another piece of wall paper and folded it very precisely so (a) I would not tread on it (b) I could hold it more easily and (c) I could see where I was going. Some hope. I dropped the whole damned thing again and, climbing down to pick it up, stepped straight into the paste bucket up to my right ankle! Avril was now in a hopeless state, in a heap, in the middle of our bed laughing uncontrollably as I blasphemed and swore that I would have nothing to do with decorating ever again. And I have never, since that day, placed my hands on, or near, pasted wallpaper. On the other hand Avril has very kindly, and skilfully, decorated every room since.

Hey Teacher, You're 'aving a Larf

As for silicone sealant—P-l-e-a-s-e! It still gives me nightmares having messed up our lovely, olive-green (well it was the Seventies!) bath. The plan was to re-silicone the bath where the old sealant had perished. I began very carefully that Saturday morning by slowly squeezing the sealant out of its tube with the sealant gun, thinking positive thoughts and reassuring myself that I could apply it to all the parts of the bath that needed it. I didn't know at the time that it would be on ALL parts of the bath, many that didn't need it! What proved fatal, and my undoing, was smoothing it down with my right index finger and then removing the surplus sealant off my finger with my other hand. The sealant was now on both hands. Rinse it off? Big mistake! Wipe it off with toilet roll? OK, now the sealant was on the toilet roll holder! Use more water? The sealant is now on the inside of the bath. Now it's on the outside of the bath panel. Now the bath panel has a hole in it! Now my wife is angry. Now no more cuddles for a week!

So it continues, but my incompetence is not only confined to home decorating. Oh no! Car maintenance is a speciality. My first car, a VW Beetle, had been in need of an oil top-up. Without studying a handbook, I felt I knew what to do, so I opened the rear end where the engine was, (it WAS a Beetle!) lifted out what appeared to be a barbecue style rod and peered at the engine. Bringing my new five litre oil-can to the car, I opened the can, pulled out the plastic pourer and attempted to pour the oil into what I thought was the correct receptacle. The pourer was much too big for the hole, so I returned to the house and made my own cardboard filter funnel, though I had to roll it very tightly at one end to fit the small hole. I returned back to the car and proceeded to decant the oil with my home-made funnel. This process was so damned slow I began to think VW were not as efficient as they claimed to be. I returned to the house for a rest and, every so often, went back to the car to pour a drop more oil into the funnel. I say a drop and I mean a drop because that was all it would take. On one of my sorties a mate, Brian Rickets, who knew a thing or two about cars appeared and asked me what the problem was with my car. When I told him about my oil decanting problem he looked at me as if I was from another planet, which I might well have been where cars were concerned. He then took out my home made filter funnel, replaced the *dipstick*, took off the main oil cap and proceeded to complete the oil top- up in seconds, with me looking on amazed. Last time I played with a car that was!

I'm sure Brian will not mind me recalling a story he told me years ago when, as a dab hand at mending cars, he was trying to sort out a car problem of his own one Saturday afternoon when his wife Janet wanted to go shopping. Arranging to pick Janet up at the shopping centre if he had mended the fault, she set off on the bus to do her chores. A couple of hours later Janet returned. Struggling past their car with the shopping and seeing legs sticking out from underneath the car's front wheels, she gave a gentle and 'friendly' tweak to the tender part between those legs. Walking down the path to the house and opening the front door she was amazed to be met by Brian who had not been able to mend the car. He had called out the AA emergency

Hey Teacher, You're 'aving a Larf

services and the mechanic was now walking down the garden path with blood pouring from a cut above the eye, having hit his head on the oil sump underneath Brian's car, when tweaked! Oh to be an A.A. man but not like the injured one at Brian's.

If not, maybe a cricketer? At least, that's what I have tried to be in my spare time for Coleshill CC having spent all my summers there since 1969. A fast bowler by trade, until age caught up with me in my late Thirties and so I could get out of bed the following day, I changed and bowled medium-paced. When various bodily problems started to appear once again I slowed my bowling right down to off-spin and began batting a little higher up the order. All those weekends spent playing and meeting with guys who are still acquaintances today ……. and now, frighteningly, I am old enough to be the Team Manager, helping the younger players, many of whom were my protégés fifteen to twenty years ago. Or in David Pudge's case, thirty years ago! Playing cricket at college I played alongside local cricketing legend and stalwart Alan 'Outy' Outram. I later played against him for our respective clubs when we both started teaching in Birmingham but were to join up and we played together once more at Coleshill until we retired from the game. I mention him because he was without doubt the best wicket keeper I ever played with. He could, and should, have played for Warwickshire and probably would have done so but for his first head teacher. Ask him about the crooked fingers on both of his hands and the expletives fly. My name is damned even further and he goes into some diatribe about how I broke most of them with crap bowling. Well we've had a few beers together after games over the years, and having both captained the Coleshill Team we always had a lot to say about the game too. Fortunately for us our wives were always incredibly understanding whilst most of our summer weekends were spent playing cricket! Happy days.

Playing football with several reasonable local teams after I left college, any serious thoughts I had of progress were shattered when I suffered a serious knee injury whilst playing in Warwick with Tamworth FC Reserves. I'd never have been any use anyway because I smoked cigarettes at that time! I finished in the Midland Combination Leagues with Whitesmore Old Boys who were a motley collection of schoolteachers and some good young students whose legs and lungs helped us 'old folks' out. I have fond memories relating to this period but not all of them good though, eh Dominick Dick Campbell?

Back in my Night school at Park Hall, in an attempt to get fit after injury one year, it was not long before the Farthings Pub Team, close by, asked me to train them, play for them and captain them. The Quinn brothers, Mr Martin Harris, several old boys from Park Hall, mates from Coleshill, big Dominick (gave him another chance) all played for a few seasons and it was so good to be amongst friends. I had to finish playing in 1972 because of my encephalitis illness and for a couple of years had to twiddle my thumbs. I decided when I recovered to give football one more shot (ha ha ha) and joined a local pub team, the Woodsman on Chelmsley Wood. The secretary and general dogsbody who served the club so well was a John Rigby who ran the team from top to bottom. A good bunch of blokes to play with, the only gripe I had was with the opposition who would insist on calling me 'granddad'! One Sunday game I remember well followed a car crash involving several of our team. In the days before mobile phones we just thought the missing players were late and would turn up eventually. They didn't and we played. We won the match narrowly and not much remained of the game in my memory apart from thinking of the chaps in the crash whose injuries, thankfully, were very slight.

Several years later I took my son Andrew in his wheelchair to watch a local cup-final under flood lights, a game my old Woodsman team were playing in. On entering the ground this bloke placed a large arm across my chest and asked me who I was, and was I who he thought I was! Are you with it so far? I asked him who wanted to know. He said his brother had played in that game when the boys had suffered the car crash and I, innocent me, had broken his brother's heart. I asked what he meant by this. In that game, so he said, his brother had headed the ball goal-wards over our keeper, and just as the ball was entering the net for his brother's first goal ever, I popped up and back-kicked it over my head and out of the goal. Even better, I hit it so hard that it went almost to the half way line where it was picked up and controlled by Kevin Hunt, the ex-Villa player who played for us, and he ran through, beat the keeper and scored at the other end! I told the bloke that it had probably been me but it was something that I did regularly, and I was sorry, I could not remember the particular incident he referred to. I should cocoa! I still dream about performing the same trick at Wembley for England, even at my age. Whoopee!

Having been involved with sport of various kinds for many years, it was always an ambition to travel abroad to see some international games. I had been lucky and I had seen plenty of games at Wembley and Edgbaston, but I had always had the urge to see England, in one guise or other, play abroad. It was not to happen in the manner I expected. I did not book the holiday to see England play cricket in South Africa. It all happened after I entered, and won, a Daily Telegraph competition where one had to guess certain results in a limited 50-over game at Lords: which players would score most runs, take most wickets and hold most catches in the game. I made my choice and entered. When a lady from some company rang to tell me I had won, I thought it was one of my 'mates' winding me up and told her so in no uncertain manner, only to 'crawl' back down the phone line five minutes later humbly apologising to the same lady for having 'completely misunderstood the situation'. We went to South Africa and Cape Town, my good friend Ian Johnson and I for twelve nights. England's team were defeated at cricket but Ian and I had a whale of a time travelling around with Gulliver's, a first class sport's tour company. I'd been left for the Grim Reaper to collect earlier that year 1995 so the holiday came as a welcome bonus. Diagnosed at home as having had a massive heart attack one night, the locum left me and my wife alone in the house until the ambulance arrived. The doctor just cleared off and left me having said he could do no more as I was beyond help. (Many people have suggested exactly the

Hey Teacher, You're 'aving a Larf

same over the years) A large pulmonary embolism was discovered which gave me many problems and scares afterwards but I'm still here……..

Since 1995 I have had to rely on prescription drugs to keep me alive. Some I have cast aside, mainly because the side effects were not helping me. Now that most of the drugs have worked most of my problems have disappeared thanks to good management by the doctors and of course the help of my family. I now get more sleep per night, not much more, but I do get past midnight now. I am able to pace myself during the day and can often get out and about on the country roads close to home cycling on my bike to chill out. At one stage, early in my illness, I could hardly walk 200 yards let alone go for a pint. Touch wood, our son Andrew, as I write, has become more manageable and although his behaviour can be challenging, we are aware that this can change at the flick of a switch. We really do now manage him better. Lastly, despite all the rages and anger I once displayed, often directed towards my family, Avril, my daughter Anna and my sisters Helen and Pamela have all stood by me through the darkest days which I know are behind me. It has not been an easy journey these last few years but without them and, of course, Ian and Stewart, I would not be here today to write this book. Thanks are not enough but for now, that is all I can offer.

Of the two good mates I have mentioned, Stewart Cooper and Ian Johnson, sadly only Stewart is alive today. He and his wife Teresa have just become grandparents for the first time, courtesy of their daughter Emma and son-in-law Peter, and baby Toby will have to support

Leeds United, poor kid! Their other daughter, Sarah, is currently teaching in Nottingham carrying on the family tradition. Having known Stewart and taught with him for most of my career, our friendship is, as the kids say, 'solid man'. There ain't much we don't know about each other and I am so grateful to have had him as a friend all these years, not only as a valuable support with Andrew, but in teaching too.

Ian Johnson came to work at Smith's Wood in 1974 and we soon became firm friends with him and his wife Nanette. We were very fortunate to share with them many memorable holidays all over the U.K., Europe and America. They often visited us on Sunday nights for a chat and game of cards and we regularly kept our kids awake as we laughed the night away. Importantly for Avril and me they were always there at the end of a phone whenever our children had medical problems. They came round to sit with one child whilst Avril and I went to the hospital with the other. A priceless, irreplaceable friendship was taken away from us all when Ian died of cancer in September 2004, a bloke whose support and friendship extended far and wide: very much the brother I never had.

Today my family is expanding, in numbers that is. Avril my wife has retired from teaching and spends her days mainly looking after all her family, including mother-in-law Peggy, our precious first grand child, Ruby Grace, born November 6th 2006, Andrew, me and any other waif and stray that enters the house. For 'relaxation' Avril spends her time in the gym or the swimming pool. Ha Ha Ha! As if she has not had

Hey Teacher, You're 'aving a Larf

enough exercise looking after us. By the way, she now has a bus pass!

Our beautiful and severely brain-damaged son Andrew will be thirty-six in March 2008 and although still a demanding and challenging 24/7, he is such a lovely bloke. He can though change from being the best friend anyone ever had – smiling, happy, compliant and full of tricks – to a rampaging, shouting, screaming adult who doesn't seem to know what he is doing - only to revert back minutes later. He still does not sleep very well. His pattern of sleep can be so completely bizarre I cannot understand how he can be so good and of course his low ability and autistic tendencies still prevail. His last assessment classified him as being as able as a ten month old baby. However, having been told by a paediatrician that he would never talk, walk or feed himself (we have taught him the latter two,) we still await his first word. God forbid he copies any of the words he hears me utter in my car as I curse all drivers under the age of sixty! Currently he attends a day unit at Brooklands Hospital, Marston Green near Birmingham, where even now he is still the 'runt of the litter'. His respite time, for which his mum and I are extremely grateful, both to the hospital and Social Services, is spent at the same unit. Regardless of all his problems he really is such a lovely handsome bloke. He is always there when I need to talk to someone impartial, and he never tells a soul what I have said!

Anna our daughter is now mum to Ruby Grace, and her fantastic husband, Mike, is a Police Inspector. Working part time for the Children's Society, Anna has developed into a very organised and efficient young mum: intelligent, articulate, funny and very talented, despite being my daughter! The two years she spent abroad with Mike in Australia, the Far East and Norway after university, certainly extended their education and helped make them 'children of the world' that they are today. (She will kill me when she reads this bit!)

My own future is very positive. My illnesses, I'd like to think, are behind me and I look forward to teaching Ruby how to play cricket, football, rugby and snakes and ladders for England of course. Avril is happy helping Anna with Ruby as much as possible. Peggy, the mum-in-law is mid-eighties, still cooks, solves crosswords and enjoys a tipple or two. The only blot could be Andrew's final placement when Avril and I can no longer care for him because of our creeping feebleness. That will without doubt, be the hardest decision of our lives and we shall face it when it comes.

Now, going full circle, you may remember I said that I was born in Sheffield at the end of the Second World War. On a visit to Australia in 1999 to see Anna and Mike when they were working in Adelaide, I met up with Steve Tracy, an old friend from Coleshill Cricket Club. I was invited to play petanque one very hot Sunday morning. You must know that French game, also known as boules. The games took place every Sunday morning following a Bacchanalian Saturday night, and Steve and many friends always chilled out on the petanque-park close to Adelaide's south side. That was my pleasure that particular morning and, following several games in the searing heat it was soon time for a cool drink. In the Exeter Pub they were serving dinner as we arrived so we bought our beers, sat at the tables on

Hey Teacher, You're 'aving a Larf

the first floor veranda and checked out the menu. By the time everyone was seated and the latecomers had arrived we'd all ordered, and some of the meals were being already being sampled. There must have been close to thirty adults at the tables. When allowed to join in the conversation, after all this was Australia, I was interrupted by a genteel voice about six places away from me asking where I hailed from since my accent was not Australian.

'The UK' I replied.

'I know that, stupid, but whereabouts in the UK?' the voice asked.

'I live in Birmingham now, but was born in Sheffield, who wants to know?' I retorted.

'Which hospital in Sheffield' the voice asked.

'You're a nosey git, why do you want to know?' I responded and that silenced the nearby conversationalists who were now about to participate in what looked like a very slow tennis match, heads swinging this way and that.

'I was born in Jessops' I continued.

'When and which year?' she asked more demandingly this time.

'Bloody hell, October nineteen forty five, what is this all about?' By now I had stopped eating but still could not identify the questioner who carried on the interrogation.

'I may have delivered you as I worked in that hospital as registrar in the delivery ward at the time of your birth,' was her next comment.

I could have fallen through the floor of the veranda to the Pub at that moment, but to the astonishment of the other guests, I stood up making as if to remove my trousers and said quietly,

'If I showed you my bottom, would recognise it?'

'My dear I don't know' she continued, 'but I probably cut off your foreskin!'

Blushing, I persisted 'But if you did, some other bugger's stitched it back on again.' And with that, the people at the nearby tables who had witnessed the exchanges stood and gave us both a round of applause. Peggy and I met several times after that, the last being in January 2003 just before her archaeological holiday to Iraq!

As they say, 'what goes around comes around' and what better example to finish with.